REVELATION

FOR

TODAY

Dr. Telford Barrett

xulon PRESS

Revelation For Today
by Dr. Telford Barrett

Printed in the United States of America

ISBN 978-1-60791-090-9

Unless otherwise indicated, Bible quotations are taken from The King James Version.

www.xulonpress.com

Introduction

The author of the Book of Revelation was the Apostle John. The Revelation was written by John when he was banished on the Isle of Patmos about 95 or 96 A.D. During the first two centuries, of the New Testament Church, there were ten different Roman Emperors who severely persecuted the Christians. The Roman Emperor, Domitian, imprisoned John to silence his preaching of the Gospel. When John was imprisoned on Patmos the Holy Spirit came upon him and moved John to write the Revelation of Jesus Christ. Historical records inform us that Domitian was assassinated in 96 A.D. and after his death perhaps John was released from his imprisonment.

It is very important, in these last days, for Christians to know what will happen, on earth, during the Tribulation Period. It is comforting to know that all born-again believers will be called out of this world, and meet the LORD in the air, before the tribulation starts. I Thessalonians 4:13-18. Every Believer needs to be informed about the terrible judgments which will be poured out upon the lost people during the Tribulation. It is urgent that Christians become dedicated soul-winners so lost people will not be left behind to experience these judgments found recorded in the Book with Seven Seals found recorded in the Book of Revelation 5:1

There are some institutions being formed today, which will be used by the Anti-Christ, to promote his agenda to overthrow God and capture the Holy City our New Jerusalem. There is now a passionate desire to rebuild the temple in Jerusalem and, in the middle of the Tribulation, the Anti-Christ will set himself up to be worshipped as a god, which is called the Abomination of Desolation; Matthew 24:15. The formation of a confederation of ten major world governments, Satan will control, is now being united into a one world government. One currency is being promoted to enhance world trade by a common market.

The Book of Revelation is to be interpreted literally, except when the statement is prefaced by the phrase "as it were", which will indicate that this is a symbol. In other places, if a symbol is used, a sincere scrutiny of the context will alert the student that a symbol is being used to convey a more clear under standing of the events of prophesy.

There are five Old Testament Books, Isaiah, Ezekiel, Daniel, Joe; and Zechariah which complement and give much information about the tribulation period. The Old Testament Prophetic writers add important information to the Book of Revelation and complete the understanding of the events during the Last Days.

Preface

A clear knowledge of he Book of Revelation is the key to the understanding of how God will destroy Satan and establish a perfect eternity for Christians.

This book has been written to inform the average church member how God will redeem the world, from Satan, and execute the plan found in the Seven Sealed Book. Conflicting views have not been discussed, which may confuse those who want to start their study of prophesy.

Each verse is recorded and then discussed with a clear teaching of the Book of Revelation.

Understanding the events, in the order in which they occur, is reassuring to every believer about the power and ability of God, to succeed in bringing the world under His complete control.

Listed below are the major events, in sequence, from the start of the Tribulation Period until the New Heaven and the New Earth are brought into existence.

1. The rapture of the church when Jesus comes in the atmosphere and calls the born-again believers to meet Him in the air. I Thessalonians 4:13-18
2. Jesus will take His believers on to Heaven, where God dwells, and for the next seven years Christians will experience the Judgment Seat and be united to Christ forever. Romans 14:10
3. There will be much confusion on earth about the disappearance of Christians from the world. I Corinthians 15:51-52.

4. The man, who will later be revealed as the antichrist, will appear as a great world leader, who convinces the world governments that he knows how to bring peace and order to a world of confusion. Revelation 6:2

5. The first seal is opened and the antichrist appears as a great peace maker. Revelation 6:1-2

6. God will call two witnesses to testify to those left to go through the tribulation. Revelation 11:3-12

7. The second seal is opened and the antichrist persuades ten nations to attack Israel who they believe is the trouble-maker in the mid-east. Revelation 6:3

8. The third seal depicts the terrible famine that follows the war described in Ezekiel 38 and 39. Revelation 6:5-6.

9. The fourth seal indicates that one fourth of the world population dies as a result of the war, hunger and by the wild beast of the earth. Revelation 6:7-8.

10. The fifth seal records the testimony of those who will be martyred in the Tribulation. Revelation 6:9-11

11. The sixth seal brings a great earthquake where the smoke fills the atmosphere. Revelation 6:12-17.

12. God calls one hundred and forty and four thousand Israelites to be evangels to preach the gospel during the tribulation. Revelation 7:3-8

13. The seventh seal reveals there will be seven more trumpet judgments to follow. Revelation 8:1-6.

14. The first angel sounds his trumpet which results in hail and fire mingled with blood to fall upon the earth. Revelation 8:7.

15. The second angel sounds and one third of the sea becomes as blood. Revelation 8:8

16. The third angel sounds and one third of the fresh water is made bitter. Revelation 8:10-11

17. The fourth angel judgment is the loss of one third of the light given from the heavenly Planets, sun and stars. Revelation 8:12

18. The fifth angel sounds his trumpet and Satan is permitted to open the bottomless pit and releases the most wicked demons upon the earth. Revelation 9:1-11.
19. The abomination of desolation and the revealing of the anti-christ take place in the middle of the tribulation. Matthew 24:15
20. The sixth angel permits four fallen evil angels to bring suffering upon man. Revelation 9:13-15.
21. The seventh angel sounds the trumpet and as a result there will be seven more judgments poured out of vials upon the earth. Revelation 10:7.
22. The first vial is poured out which results in a painful and grievous sore to be upon those who have taken the mark of the beast. Revelation 16:2.
23. The second vial causes the sea to become blood as that of a dead man. Revelation 16:3.
24. The third vial causes all fresh water to become blood. Revelation 16:4.
25. The fourth vial poured out upon the sun results in the increase of heat to burn people with blisters. Revelation 16:8-9
26. The fifth vial causes the world to become totally dark. Revelation 16:10
27. The sixth vial dries up the Euphrates River so the kings of the East may invade Israel. Revelation 16:12
28. The seventh angel brings to pass the judgment of the apostate religions of the world. Revelation 17:1-18.
29. An angel from Heaven destroys Babylon. Revelation 18:1-24.
30. Satan and his army is destroyed. Revelation 19:15-19.
31. The beast and false prophet are cast into Hell. Revelation 19:2
32. Satan, the old serpent, is banished into the bottomless pit for one thousand years. Revelation 20:1-3.
33. Jesus brings in the Millennium and rules the world from the re-established throne of David in Jerusalem. Revelation 21:1-27.

34. The New Jerusalem is established upon the new earth and will be the eternal dwelling place for the redeemed of all ages. Revelation 22:1-5

Chapter I

Introduction: John the Beloved wrote this book about 95 or 96 A.D. Chapter one gives a revelation of our risen Lord Jesus Christ in His Glorified body in Heaven. The illustrious form Jesus now possesses is described in verses 13 -15, and it will be the same body Jesus will have when He returns to call the church out of this world to meet Him in the air.

1. *The Revelation of Jesus Christ, which God gave unto him, to shew unto his servants things which must shortly come to pass; and he sent and signified it by his angel unto his Servant John.*

    The Holy Spirit breathed upon John the Beloved to write this Revelation of Jesus Christ. John was instructed about things which must shortly come to pass; meaning that when the tribulation period starts that the length of time of seven years will soon come to an end. An angel of God confirmed to John the truth about what he is writing.

2. *Who bare record of the word of God, and of the testimony of Jesus Christ, and of all things that he saw.*

    The Holy Spirit moved John the Beloved to give his testimony that he had personally been with Jesus; who is the Word of God. John 1:14 defines Jesus as being the word of God, "And the Word was made flesh, and dwelt among us, (and we beheld his glory, the glory as of the only begotten of the Father,) full of grace and truth."

John, also, had the joyous privilege, during the three and one half years of Jesus' earthly ministry, of beholding the Son of God and seeing the miracles Jesus performed.

3. *Blessed is he that readeth, and they that hear the word of this prophecy, and keep those things which are written therein: for the time is at hand.*

A blessing is promised to every one who reads or studies this book of the Bible. Many truths are given about future events that will strengthen the faith of believers by knowing how God will finally end Satan's power over man and the casting of Satan into the Lake of Fire. Blessed is every believer who permits this book of Revelation to guide them into Spiritual maturity.

4. *John to the seven churches which are in Asia: Grace be unto you, and peace, from him which is, and which was, and which is to come; and from the seven Spirits which are before the throne;*

The Seven Churches in Asia are addressed to receive the blessings of divine love and peace from the eternal and everlasting God. The second coming of Jesus is again promised in this verse. The Seven Spirits of God are found listed in Isaiah 11:2-3:

> 2. "And the spirit of the Lord shall rest upon him, the spirit of wisdom and understanding, the spirit of counsel and might, the spirit of knowledge and of the fear of the Lord.
> 3. And shall make him of quick understanding in the fear of the LORD: and he shall not judge after the sight of his eyes, neither reprove after the hearing of his ears."

These seven spirits are the different departments of the working of the Holy Spirit who carries out the commands of God. These seven functions of the Holy Spirit always protect the Throne of God from any intrusion of evil that Satan may attempt to use against God.

5. *And from Jesus Christ, who is the faithful witness, and the first begotten of the dead, and the prince of the kings of the earth. Unto him that loved us, and washed us from our sins in his own blood. And from Jesus Christ, who is the faithful witness, and the first begotten of the dead, and the*

Jesus Christ was, for three and one half years, a faithful witness of truth to all mankind. His faithful witness originated from his attribute of omniscience. The first begotten of the dead was the resurrection of Jesus from the grave with a glorified eternal body. The first resurrection indicated that there will be a great harvest of his believers rising from the grave. True believers will be given a glorified body like the one Jesus received when He was resurrected on Easter Sunday morning. At this time the rapture of the Church will take place and the Tribulation will begin.

After the Tribulation has ended, John speaks of the "prince of the kings of the earth". Here he is telling of the time when Jesus will establish his throne in Jerusalem. This signifies the beginning of Christ's millennial rule on earth. The king who sits upon the Throne of David will be the same ruler who loved us with a divine love we call grace and redeemed us with the atonement made by the shedding of his blood at Calvary.

6. *And hath made us kings and priests unto God and his Father; to him be glory and dominion for ever and ever. Amen.*

When sinners are saved and born into God's family, by the spiritual birth, this places them as a ruler and minister ruling and reigning with Christ, upon this earth, during the Millennium. The Glory of Jesus Christ is the radiance that shines forth from his Attribute of Holiness.

7. *Behold, he cometh with clouds; and every eye shall see him, and they also which pierced him: and all kindreds of the earth shall wail because of him. Even so, Amen.*

Jesus will draw near to the earth to call his Church to meet him in the air. Paul corroborates this truth in I Thessalonians 4:17, "Then we which are alive and remain shall be caught up together with them in the clouds, to meet the Lord in the air, and so shall we ever be with the Lord."

This second coming, recorded in verse seven of Revelation, must be at the time of Christ's revealing of himself to man at the end of the Tribulation. By the use of television and other media, the world will be able to witness His return. At the same time, coming with clouds, will be the heavenly army of saints, the true believers who received a new body at the beginning of the rapture. This army will be, the New Testament Church, clothed with white garments riding upon white horses approaching the earth from heaven.

When Jesus draws near to the earth and stands upon the Mount of Olives, the whole world, including Israel, will see the crucified Lord.

Zechariah.14:4, "And his feet shall stand in that day upon the Mount of Olives, which is before Jerusalem on the east...."Zechariah. 12:10, "And I will pour upon the house of David, and upon the inhabitants of Jerusalem, the spirit of grace and of supplications: and they shall look upon me whom they have pierced, and they shall mourn for him, as one mourneth for his only son, and shall be in bitterness for his firstborn." The cry of anguish will be because the world shall know for certain that the Saviour, who was crucified, was their Lord whom they rejected.

8. *I am Alpha and Omega, the beginning and the ending, saith the Lord, which is, and which was, and which is to come, the Almighty.*

At this point John turns from prophecy to recounting what he witnessed in the Lord's presence. This verse declares the Lord Jesus to be the eternal God. Jesus will return, at the end

14

of the tribulation period, to establish the millennial kingdom upon the earth. The Almighty, the all sufficient One, will rule during the millennium from the Throne of David which will be reestablished in Jerusalem.

9. *I John, who also am your brother, and companion in tribulation, and in the kingdom and patience of Jesus Christ, was in the isle that is called Patmos, for the word of God, and for the testimony of Jesus Christ.*

Domitian was the Emperor of Rome from 81 to 96 A.D. During his fifteen year reign Domitian banished John, to the small desolate island of Patmos in the Aegean Sea, for preaching the gospel. Rome considered the preaching of the gospel about Jesus to be a crime. In this verse John identifies himself, as a brother, to all believers who have endured trials and persecutions for their witnessing for Jesus Christ.

10. *I was in the Spirit on the Lord's day, and heard behind me a great voice, as of a trumpet,*

The Lord's day could very well be the first day of the week that Paul made reference to in I Corinthians 16:2, "Upon the first day of the week let every one of you lay by him in store, as God hath prospered him, that there be no gatherings when I come."

The trumpet referred to in verse ten doesn't mean a literal trumpet because it was prefaced by the words, "as of." The study of the book of Revelation is to be taken literally unless indicated by the introduction of the phrase "as it were" or "as of." The voice of Jesus speaks with authority as a trumpet would be used by an army to call troops into battle. Jesus speaks to John proclaiming His authority.

11. *Saying, I am Alpha and Omega, the first and the last; and, What thou seest, write in a book, and send it unto the seven churches which are in Asia; unto Ephesus, and unto Smyrna, and unto Pergamos, and unto Thyatira, and unto Sardis, and unto Philadelphia, and unto Laodicea.*

Again, John is identifying the One who speaks, as a trumpet, to be the Lord Jesus Christ the eternal and ever-lasting God. The message of this book, the redemption of the earth, is to be sent to the seven churches in Asia listed as Ephesus, Smyrna, et al.

12. *And I turned to see the voice that spake with me. And being turned, I saw seven golden candlesticks.*

The sound of the voice John heard moved him to turn to see the One who was speaking. In verse eleven the seven golden candlesticks represented the seven churches who will receive the book of Revelation. Gold is a precious metal identified with Royalty. This first view in Heaven reveals to John that Jesus considers His church to be precious and valuable in His sight. A candle or lamp stand depicts the church as a shining light to a world in darkness.

13. *And in the midst of the seven candlesticks one like unto the Son of man, clothed with a garment down to the foot, and girt about the paps with a golden girdle.*

Jesus is seen in the center of His churches that He died for on the cross. The long priestly garment designates Jesus as High Priest for all who make up His church. The golden girdle, worn by kings, wrapped around the waist, reveals Christ to be the king of kings, who will rule on the earth during the millennium.

14. *His head and his hairs were white like wool, as white as snow; and his eyes were as a flame of fire;*

The nation of Israel chose the aged men to sit in counsel or to hold the court trials in Old Testament days. The gray hairs of mature men indicated one of experience and intelligence. Ascribing to Jesus, the risen and glorified Lord, this quality of white hair as white as snow is to be the intelligence of omniscience. As a flame of fire indicates that the eyes of Jesus are not a literal flame of fire. As heat penetrates an entire object so does the eyes of Jesus penetrate the veneer of our soul and see us as we really are. Nothing can be hidden from our Lord.

15. *And his feet like unto fine brass, as if they burned in a furnace; and his voice as the sound of many waters.*

One of the promises God made to Abraham was all the land that he walked upon would be given to him in fulfillment of a covenant made with him in the land of Ur. In the book of II Chronicles 4:1 Solomon made an alter of brass for the Temple as a place where sin is judged. The feet of Jesus represent Him taking this world back under His control in judgment during the seven years of the Tribulation. Fine brass refers to judgment that is pure and righteous. The smelting of brass in the furnace separates the pure brass from all other impurities. The voice of Jesus, like many waters of a rushing torrent, cannot be stopped. No man, not even Satan, can hold back the judgment process of Jesus as required in the Seven Sealed Book. The Seven Sealed Book will be addressed in chapter five.

16. *And he had in his right hand seven stars; and out of his mouth went a sharp two-edged sword: and his countenance was as the sun shineth in his strength.*

The holding of the seven ministers in His hand reveals the loving care Jesus has for His servants. The sword out of His mouth is the Word of God that stands forever unchanged. The result of the use of the sword is found in Hebrews 4:12 "For the word of God is quick, and powerful, and sharper than any two-edged sword, piercing even to the dividing asunder of soul and spirit, and of the joints and marrow, and is a discerner of the thoughts and intents of the heart."

His countenance is the radiance of His Glory which shines forth from His Holiness. John describes the brilliance of this countenance to be brighter than the sun shining at noon.

17. *And when I saw him, I fell at his feet as dead. And he laid his right hand upon me, saying unto me, Fear not; I am the first and the last*:

John was so over-whelmed when he saw the brightness of the shechinah, an indescribable glory, of the risen Lord that he fell at His feet as if stricken dead. Placing the right hand upon the head of John was an act of comfort and security in the presence of Jesus. Often the Holy Spirit will move John to establish the truth about Jesus being the eternal God.

18. *I am he that liveth, and was dead; and, behold, I am alive for evermore, Amen; and have the keys of hell and of death.*

Jesus declares that He came to this earth as the son of man in order that He may have a physical body capable of dying on the cross. The atonement was necessary to bring salvation to sinful man. Being alive for evermore is a declaration Jesus gave that He will remain in His glorified resurrected body forever. Believers will forever have, in Heaven, the evidence that Jesus died for our sins and saved us by His grace. Having the keys indicates that Jesus has the power to reject Satan and all who follow him and banish them in the lake of fire.

19. *Write the things which thou hast seen, and the things which are and the things which shall be hereafter;*

One of the things John saw was the Lord Jesus Christ in His glorified body in Heaven, as recorded in chapter one. The things recorded in chapters two and three are applicable to the seven churches in Asia. John then resumes with prophecy telling of things to come in chapter four and continues to the end of the book of Revelation.

20. *The mystery of the seven stars which thou sawest in my right hand, and the seven golden candlesticks. The seven stars are the angels of the seven churches: and the seven candlesticks which thou sawest are the seven churches.*

John is giving to the student of this book a key of understanding to unlock the mystery about the seven stars identified as the angels or messengers of God in the churches of Asia and throughout the church period. The angels of the churches are understood to be the same as the pastors who preach the Word of God. The candlesticks represent the church to be the light of the world.

CHAPTER II

Introduction: John was instructed, in chapter 1:4, to write to the seven churches in Asia. Some of the churches received commendations and others received a rebuke. This chapter contains the churches that existed from the first century to the end of the 1400's. There is a good possibility that each of these churches represent seven different church periods.

1. **Unto the angel of the church of Ephesus write; These things saith he that holdeth the seven stars in his right hand, who walketh in the midst of the seven golden candlesticks;**

The angel of the church of Ephesus is the messenger, or pastor, of the church of Ephesus. This church existed during the first century of Christianity. It is believed that Paul was there for three years. He that holdeth, or controls, the seven pastors is the Lord Jesus Christ. Holding the pastors in the Lord's right hand reveals His protective care and love for them. Jesus who is walking in the midst of the churches is judging each church.

2. **I know thy works, and thy labour, and thy patience, and how thou canst not bear them which are evil: and thou hast tried them which say they are apostles, and are not, and hast found them liars:**

Jesus said that He knew of their many church activities and dedicated work in the church. Jesus expects Christians to be active in all church functions, but more than works, He desires their love and fellowship. The church at Ephesus has been patient with those who opposed the believers and did evil things against them. The loving Christian testimony was never compromised to becoming evil toward the evil doers. This church at Ephesus was praised for being diligent in their investigation of some, who wanted to identify with the church body, but they were still lost in their sins. Obviously, some sinful people had lied to the church and were seeking to be added to the church membership before they were converted.

3. **And hast borne, and hast patience, and for my name's sake hast laboured, and hast not fainted.**

   The patients of the saints at Ephesus were noted for their quality of continually dealing with problems of persecution for years without failing in their Christian testimony. Moreover, the believers continued to work regardless of persecution so they may glorify the name of the Lord Jesus as their Saviour. In many ways this church at Ephesus was an ideal church in serving the Lord.

4. **Nevertheless I have some-what against thee, because thou hast left thy first love.**

   The Lord was more concerned about their love and devotion to Him more than their diligent works for the church. The quality of love that was waning was a divine love named "agape" in the Greek text. "Agape" love is more that human affection for the family; it is a divine quality of love which is imparted to Christians as a result of God's love being shed abroad in the hearts of all believers.

5. **Remember therefore from whence thou art fallen, and repent, and to the first works; or else I will come unto thee quickly, and will remove thy candlestick out of his place, except thou repent.**

This statement proclaims Jesus to be the one who died on the cross and was raised in a glorified resurrected body

The Holy Spirit moved John to challenge the church at Ephesus to think about the pure love they experienced when they were first saved, and return to loving the Lord as He had loved them. This church was cautioned to turn from a life of works only, and love the Savior first, and then work because of that love relationship. The warning was that if they did not repent, and turn back to proper worship, their church would cease to be a soul-winning church and not be a light for the lost world to follow.

6. **But this thou hast, that thou hatest the deeds of the Nicolaitans, which I also hate.**

The church at Ephesus had a common dislike for the Nicolaitans, which the Lord Jesus said that He also hated. The word "Nicolaitans" came from two Greek words, "nikao"-to conquer and "Laos"- the people. The combining of the two words had the meaning of the clergy who ruled over the members of the church body.

7. *He that hath an ear, let him hear what the Spirit saith unto the churches; To him that over-cometh will I give to eat of the tree of life, which is in the midst of the paradise of God.*

If anyone has an ear, be sure to listen attentively to what is being said, because this is important. The important message to the churches is those born again believers who remain true to the Lord will eat from the tree of life in Heaven. There was a tree of life in the Garden of Eden, and those who ate of this tree would never die. The Lord promised all resurrected believers to have access to the tree of life, in Heaven, and live forever.

8. *And unto the angel of the church in Smyrna, write; These things saith the first and the last, which was dead, and is alive;*

The Smyrna church period can be dated from about 100 A.D. to 316 A.D. At the end of this period a Roman Emperor Constantine came to power. Constantine, in 312 A.D., embraced the Roman church in a church and state union. The Lord Jesus once again reiterates that He is the eternal and everlasting God by His statement of being the first and the last..The Deity of Christ was affirmed by Him being raised from the grave with a glorified body.

9. *I know thy works, and tribulation, and poverty, (but thou art rich) and I know the blasphemy of them which say they are Jews, and are not, but are the synagogue of Satan.*

The Smyrna church was also a working church. Smyrna endured ten of the most dreadful times of Roman persecution the church has ever endured. The poverty left the church in a destitute state of need for material things and the necessities of life. Although, the church was experiencing poverty they, at the same time were rich in spiritual growth and maturity. There were many Jews, who were zealous for the Law of the Old Testament, who continually harassed the church because they thought the church was a new heresy to be destroyed. The informed Jews of that day were spiritually alert and recognized that Jesus was the promised Messiah who was prophesied by the Old Testament Prophets. These Judaizers had permitted Satan to influence them to believe they were the only true followers of God.

10. *Fear none of those things which thou shalt suffer: behold, the devil shall cast some of you into prison, that ye may be tried; and ye shall have tribulation ten days: be thou faithful unto death, and I will give thee a crown of life.*

The Apostle John was suffering persecution at the time he was writing the book of Revelation. The persecution continued until the end of the reign of Diocletian in 305 A.D. The number of Christians who died from the ten different Roman persecutions is unknown, although, records indicate thousands died. Those believers who remain faithful, in their

24

Christian testimony, will be granted a crown of life. The five different crowns, that may be earned, will be granted to Christians at the time of the Judgment Seat in Heaven. II Corinthians 5:10 "For we must all appear before the judgment seat of Christ; that every one may receive the things done in his body, according to that he hath done, whether it be good or bad."

11. *He that hath an ear, let him hear what the Spirit saith unto the churches; He that overcometh shall not be hurt of the second death.*

If anyone has the capacity to hear, make sure you listen carefully to what follows in this verse. The important statement is to the Christians at Smyrna about enduring persecution and if you experience death you have nothing to fear in relation to the second death. A second death occurs to the lost person when they are judged, at the Great White Throne Judgment, and then cast into Hell. Physical death is the first death the lost person experiences and the second death occurs when they are eternally cut off from the grace of God and then cast into the Lake of Fire.

12. *And to the angel of the church in Pergamos write; These things saith he which hath the sharp sword with two edges;*

Pergamos represents the church age from about 316 to 500 A.D. Constantine in 313 A.D. formed a union of church and state. A union of church and state opened the door for pagan ritual to be adopted along with Christian theology.

The message is to the pastor or angel of the church at Pergamos. Jesus states that what He speaks is the Word of God. Chapter 1:16 informs the church that the two-edged sword out from His mouth is the word of God, according to Hebrews 4:12.

13. *I know thy works and where thou dwellest, even where Satan's seat is: and thou holdest fast my name, and hast*

not denied my faith, even in those days wherein Antipas was my faithful martyr, who was slain among you, where Satan dwelleth.

Jesus mentions their works and also they lived in a wicked world even where the seat, or throne, of Satan exists. During this time of severe persecution, these Christians were never ashamed of being identified as followers of the Lord Jesus. The enduring faith of this church supported Christians through much suffering. It is obvious that Antipas was a man with a deep and steadfast faith when the followers of Satan killed him.

14. *But I have a few things against thee, because thou hast there them that hold the doctrine of Balaam, who taught Balac to cast a stumblingblock before the children of Israel, to eat things sacrificed unto idols, and to commit fornication.*

The doctrine, or teaching, of Balaam is found in Numbers 22-25. Balaam led the children of Israel to inter-marry with the heathen women of Moab; who would lead the men of Israel to worship idol gods. Satan is once again encouraging the church at Pergamos to compromise their faith and visit the temples with idols and eat meat that had been offered to idol gods. Christians who visit temples of immorality, and ate meat which had been sacrificed to idol gods, would cause many other believers to stumble or question their faith in God. Sexual immorality was a common practice in the pagan temples and Christians should never be found in this place of paganism.

15. *So hast thou also them that hold the doctrine of the Nicolaitans, which thing I hate.*

The Nicolatans were those who set themselves over the common people, to rule over the populace and to dominate their lives. The Nicolaitans, also, held to the doctrine of Balaam which included immorality and tolerance to all types of human vices which excite the flesh. Jesus clearly stated that dominate control over others was something He hated.

16. ***Repent; or else I will come unto thee quickly, and will fight against them with the sword of my mouth.***

The church of Pergamos is called to repent of the sins which were found in the Nicolaitans and had become part of the activities of the clergy and laity. The strong word "repent" with a firm threat of judgment against them indicated the seriousness of their sins against the people and against God. In the book of Hebrews 4:12 the Holy Spirit breathed upon the writer to indicate that the Word of God was like a sword that cuts deep into the soul of man. Another verse that warns of the judgment of God against wickedness is found in II Thessalonians 2:8 "And then shall that Wicked be revealed, whom the Lord shall consume with the spirit of his mouth, and shall destroy with the brightness of his coming":

17. ***He that hath an ear, let him hear what the Spirit saith unto the churches; To him that overcometh will I give to eat of the hidden manna, and will give him a white stone, and in the stone a new name written, which no man knoweth saving he that receiveth it.***

The promise found in this verse is perhaps given to all churches that repent and follow the will of God. Every soul who repents and accepts Jesus as their Lord and Saviour may look forward to receiving these blessings, when they are called to meet the Lord Jesus in Heaven. Again the Lord Jesus calls believers to listen carefully to what He is about to say. The emphasis is to pay attention with alertness. Those that overcome are believers who are trusting by faith in the Lord Jesus to save and keep them. It appears that those who have been born again will feast upon some kind of heavenly food in Heaven. The Hebrew children referred to heavenly food as manna. Exodus 15:14. "And when the dew that lay was gone up, behold, upon the face of the wilderness there lay a small round thing, as small as the hoar frost on the ground. 15. And when the children of Israel saw it, they said one to another, it is manna: for Israel did not recognize what it was. And Moses said unto them, this is the bread which the Lord hath given you to eat."

No one knows what this food will be or what it will taste like; it will be something the Lord will prepare for His Saints in Heaven. Many delights are awaiting Christians, in Heaven, which could have never entered the mind of believers who are still alive on this earth.

A person who was found guilty in the courts during the Old Testament Period would be given a black stone indicating the decision of the court. When a person who was being tried for some crime was found not guilty he was given a white stone. All believers will be given a white stone in heaven, and will never be found guilty, because the blood of Jesus cleansed their soul from all of their sins. Inscribed in the white stone will be a secret name that will only be known by you and the Lord Jesus. The new name perhaps will be a name which describes something about you which the Lord Jesus finds to be precious as His Bride.

18. *And unto the angel of the church in Thyatira write; These things saith the Son of God, who hath his eyes like unto a flame of fire, and his feet are like fine brass;*

The church at Thyatira represents the church age from 500-1500 A.D. In history this was called the Dark Ages when Catholicism was the dominant church, who ruled over all nations and rulers. During this time in history the church fell to a very low degree of conduct which severely oppressed the citizens of Europe. Any person, during the dark ages, who dared to oppose Rome was dealt with by the Inquisition and most often was put to death by burning them at the stake.

The Holy Spirit directed John to restate the qualities of the attributes of Jesus which were recorded in Revelation 1:14-15. With the eyes of Jesus He is able to see all things and nothing is hidden from the Lord Jesus. The feet of Brass assures mankind that the judgments, by our lord, will be on the basis of justice and will not deviate one degree from what the Word of God has given in the Bible. The Lord Jesus will always deal with man on the basis of mercy if he will repent and trust Jesus to be his Saviour.

19. *I know thy works, and charity, and service, and faith, and thy patience, and thy works; and the last to be more than the first.*

The church of Thyatira was commended for its good works, mentioned twice, in this one verse. The service was toward helping each other, and most likely community service, in their area. Faith was noted as a commendable characteristic of the church. Because of the many adversaries, the church had to be patient in order to survive the harassment from the enemies of Christanity. The most effective out-reach of the church could have been good works of service to others in need.

20. *Not withstanding I have a few things against thee, because thou sufferest that woman Jezebel, which calleth herself a prophetess, to teach and to seduce my servants to commit fornication, and to eat things secrifieced unto idols.*

The name Jezebel often identifies pagan worship, idolatry, and even immorality as a part of their pagan ritual. This prophetess, some have identified to be Mariolatry, led the servants of God to forsake true worship of God to worship idol gods. Feasting upon meat that had been offered to pagan idols was considered not appropriate for Christian conduct and their testimony, to be separated from worldliness. Eating meat offered to idols identified that individual as one who supported idol sacrifices, by participating in their feasts.

21. *And I gave her space to repent of her fornication; and she repented not.*

Jezebel was given time to repent but she did not repent of her sins as listed in the previous verse. In like manner, the church at Thyatira will not repent of the evil that is evident, and because of this judgment will be certain. God extends mercy to all who will repent and all who rebel against God are destined to experience the wrath of God.

22. *Behold, I will cast her into a bed, and them that commit adultery with her into great tribulation, except they repent of their deeds.*

    The casting into bed is a place where adultery may be committed. Adultery brings much suffering of disease and problems that have no solution. Some Bible teachers believe that the Jezebel type of adultery is a form of worship of Mary, as a mediator, instead of Jesus being the only mediator between God and man. The church at Thyatira turned away from the true worship of God and committed spiritual adultery by adopting alien worship of idols.

23. *And I will kill her children with death; and all the churches shall know that I am he which searcheth the reins and hearts: and I will give unto every one of you according to your works.*

    Her children are the church members of this church who did not repent of their false worship and will experience rejection by the Lord at the Great White Throne Judgment and then they will be cast into the lake of fire. Jesus is omniscient and knows all things about every person. The reins are the depths of thoughts of the mind. The heart would include the emotional intents of the soul. Jesus knows the thoughts and intents of every lost person and they will be punished for all the sins they ever committed. The degree of punishment will be in the realm of mental anguish of the soul, in the Lake of Fire, we call Hell. The physical suffering will be the same for all who are cast into Hell.

24. *But unto you I say, and unto the rest in Thyatira, as many as have not this doctrine, and which have not known the depths of Satan, as they speak; I will put upon you none other burden*

There were some Christians, in the church at Thyatira, who had not been led astray and embraced false teaching, known as cults today.. The followers of Satan are embracing demon worship, in some form, by denying the Lord as God and Saviour. None other burden is a promise of Jesus that the true believers will not endure the judgment pronounced upon those who had identified themselves as followers of a Jezebel mode of idol worship.

25. *But that which ye have already hold fast till I come.*

That which ye have is the Word of God and the Gospel of Salvation, by Grace through Faith in the Son of God. Holding fast is the grasping hold upon the truth and never relinquishing the truth. Till I come is an uncertain time set for the future when Jesus will return to the earth, for His Bride, the New Testament Church.

26. *And he that overcometh, and keepeth my works unto the end, to him will I give power over the nations:*

Overcoming is attributed to believers who are faithful followers of the Lord. The works are those things the Lord Jesus commanded His children to do, as found recorded in the Bible. Jesus will return to the earth, at the end of the tribulation period, and establishes his millennial kingdom; We the Saints of God will rule and reign with Christ in His government over the earth.

27. *And he shall rule them with a rod of iron; as the vessels of a potter shall they be broken to shivers: even as I received of my Father.*

The rule of our Lord on the earth will not be that of a despot but the leading of a shepherd. The rod or scepter of iron will be firm judgment according to what is written in the Word of God. The illustration used is any attempt, in the Millennium, to do wrong will be crushed as if you would strike a peace of pottery with a rod of iron. The Lord Jesus will carry out the will of God the Father as given in the Holy Bible.

28. *And I will give him the morning star.*

The crowning joy of the Church is to have Jesus as their Bridegroom. Jesus is the morning star as recorded in Revelation 22:16 "I Jesus have sent mine angel to testify unto you these things in the churches. I am the root and the offspring of David, and the bright and morning star."

29. *He that hath an ear, let him hear what the Spirit saith unto the churches.*

Again The Holy Spirit instructs John to inform the readers of the Book of Revelation to pay close attention to every thing written in this book The emphasis is that every word is very important, so, be sure to pay attention to what is said in this book.

Chapter III

Introduction: The last three churches, Sardis, Philadelphia, and Laodicea, describe the churches that existed during and after the Reformation Period. The Sardis period was a time of doctrinal debate and formulating church doctrine. The Philadelphia period experienced great revivals in Europe and America. Many missionaries were sent around the world with evangelism and establishing churches. The Laodicean period, of the last days, of the church age, has become complacent with their wealth and comfort. The church has now lost its passion for lost souls and it is failing to lead them to know Jesus as their personal Saviour. The Laodicean church receives the strongest warning, from the Lord Jesus, informing the churches that they would be rejected by the Lord.

1. *And unto the angel of the church in Sardis write; These things saith he that hath the seven Spirits of God, and the seven stars; I know thy works, that thou hast a name that thou livest, and art dead.*

    Jesus is addressing this letter to the messengers, or pastors, of the Sardis Church. The Seven Spirits of God are discussed in Chapter 1:4. Again the Seven Spirits are mentioned to emphasize the seven departments of ministry by the Holy Spirit. The ministry of the Holy Spirit assures us that nothing can invade Heaven and overthrow God and His Heavenly Angels. The seven stars, also, refers to the pastors of these seven churches. The Sardis Church is recognized as being alive, or existing at this period, but spiritually they are inactive in reaching out to convert the world. The church leaders were so busy in setting forth their doctrine, as recorded in the Bible, that evangelism was not active in practice.

2. *Be watchful, and strengthen the things which remain, that are ready to die: for I have not found thy works perfect before God.*

The Sardis church was challenged to be alert about what needs to be done in fulfilling the commission Jesus gave to His ministers. Much had been achieved in developing Bible Doctrine, for the newly developing church bodies during the Reformation. To strengthen was to define their Bible Doctrine and have a better understanding of Scripture, which was necessary, for Spiritual maturity of the believers. The church was on the verge of closing because the members were dieing and not being replaced with new converts. Their works were not perfect because it was not a balanced ministry of Biblical instruction and Soul Winning.

3. *Remember therefore how thou hast received and heard, and hold fast, and repent. If therefore thou shalt not watch, I will come on thee as a thief, and thou shalt not know what hour I will come upon thee.*

Sardis had received the Gospel which they had heard from those who had been with the apostles. The church is commanded to carefully adhere to the truth they had learned from the apostles. The church body was to repent because of their neglect of evangelism. Our Lord considers soul winning as a most important part of the worship service. If the Sardis church fails to follow the leading of the Holy Spirit they will be judged by God at a moment when they least expect His correction.

4. *Thou hast a few names even in sardis which have not defiled their garments; and they shall walk with me in white: for they are worthy.*

A few faithful servants of God were found in the church at Sardis; Some Christians were being obedient to the teaching of the Apostles and faithful in the preaching of the Gospel. Defiled garments signify those believers who participate in sinful practices associated with the life style of the lost. Soiled garments depict a heart that is contaminated with sin of rebellion against the will of God for your life. The promise is to those faithful servants of God who will some day walk in the presence of our Lord clothed with the white garments of Heaven. The reason these followers of Jesus are worthy is because their soul has been cleansed with the atonement made by Jesus by the shedding of His blood at Calvary. The Believer could never be worthy of salvation because he is unable to save himself. Salvation is a gift from God and cannot be earned by good works.

5. *He that overcometh, the same shall be clothed in white raiment; and I will not blot out his name out of the book of life, but I will confess his name before my Father, and before his angels.*

Those who overcome are those who place their faith in Jesus and receive Him into their soul, or heart, as their Saviour and Lord. The white garments of Heaven will be a color that will glow with whiteness. In Revelation 20:12 two different books are found in Heaven. One book records all human beings who have been physically born and whether or not they are alive or deceased. The other book records the name of the person who has trusted Jesus to save them. Moses asked the Lord to blot his name out of the book of life where he is recorded and numbered among the living. Exodus 32:32 "Yet now, if thou wilt forgive their sin—; and if not, blot me, I pray thee, out of thy book which thou hast written." Moses was frustrated with the complaining of the children of Israel and God told Moses that He would kill all of them and start another nation of people who would worship Him; Moses responded to God and informed God if He had to destroy Israel to also kill him and this would take his name out of the book of life, which indicates that he was still numbered among the living. Jesus is saying that all believers will be announced as children of God before The Heavenly Father and to all the angels who dwell there.

6. *He that hath an ear, let him hear what the Spirit saith unto the churches*.

The message that Jesus has given to the church at Sardis is so important that every one who reads this book should pay close attention to what Jesus is instructing this church to do. The message to the Sardis church is also a guide and warning to all churches and Christians as to what the Lord Jesus expects of each of us.

7. *And to the angel of the church in Philadelphia write; These things saith he that is holy, he that is true, he that hath the key of David, he that openeth, and no man shutteth; and shutteth, and no man openeth*;

The Philadelphia Church represents the church age from 1750 to 1900. This period of time is known as the Great Awakening where great revivals were held and many people were saved in Europe and America. Missionaries were sent into many countries where the gospel had never been preached and many souls were born again and forgiven of all their sins.

Jesus sets forth the declaration that he who is speaking is holy, the source of all truth, which are the attributes of Deity. Jesus has a genealogy record in the Gospel of Matthew and Luke which establishes a record that Jesus is the rightful heir to the throne of David. During the Millennium, Jesus will set up the throne of David and rule the world from Jerusalem for one thousand years. The key of David signifies that Jesus has the authority to rule from the Throne of David. Isaiah 22:22 "And the key of the house of David will I lay upon his shoulder; so he shall open, and none shall shut; and he shall shut, and none shall open." Jesus is the only one who will qualify to re-establish the throne of David.

8. *I know thy works: behold, I have set before thee an open door, and no man can shut it: for thou hast a little strength, and hast kept my word, and hast not denied my name.*

Jesus is very commendable when speaking about the church at Philadelphia. This church has been faithful to preach the Word of God in the local church and minister to those who are considered to be a mission field. During this time missionaries were found willing to go to the foreign fields and, in response, the Lord Jesus moved to open those nations to accept missionaries. Some rulers of nations opposed foreigners into their country, but God moved to let missionaries enter and minister the Gospel to the lost people. Man had no ability to open foreign nations for missions; God only could open these nations for missions.

Two outstanding qualities of Christian character were found in the Philadelphia church. First, the church had heard the Word of God and made a commitment to be obedient to what they had learned through the instruction of the Holy Spirit. Second, the church was not ashamed of the Lord Jesus and openly proclaimed the Gospel to those who would listen to the preaching of God's Word.

9. *Behold, I will make them of the synagogue of Satan, which say they are Jews, and are not, but do lie; behold, I will make them to come and worship before thy feet, and to know that I have loved thee.*

Those who claim to be religious but do not know the Lord Jesus as their Saviour are in the camp of Satan. The Lord included that even the Jews, who still hold to the law, are now lost and belong to Satan, unless they come to the Lord Jesus by faith. Some time in the future, all who stand before the Great White Throne, in judgment, will know that the way to Heaven is through the atonement made by Jesus on the cross. All unsaved who are called before the Lord Jesus in Judgment will learn that Jesus loved them and died for them on the cross.

10. *Because thou hast kept the word of my patience, I also will keep thee from the hour of temptation, which shall come upon all the world, to try them that dwell upon the earth.*

Jesus promised to keep the patient Philadelphian Believers because of their faithfulness, in times of temptation. One of the outstanding evidences of a Christians faith is their being patient during times of adversity. Some Christians, who are weak in faith, fail to be patient in times of difficulty and become a detriment to their Christian testimony.

Keeping them from the hour of temptation could be a promise to all believers that they will not go through the tribulation period, which will start soon after the church is caught up to meet Jesus in the air. The tribulation period will encompass the whole world and every one left to go into the tribulation will suffer the judgments that will follow. The severity of problems caused by the judgments will be an experience no one can endure without sufferings.

11. *Behold, I come quickly: hold that fast which thou hast, that no man take thy crown.*

Jesus promised that He will come much sooner than man expects Him to return. The outstanding qualities of their faith are those the Lord Jesus encourages them to continue faithfully throughout the church age. Rewards given in the form of a crown will be granted at the Judgment Seat for the Christians. The very next event in prophesy will be the rapture of the church which will carry us into Heaven; the Judgment Seat will soon follow where rewards will be given to those who have been faithful.

12. *Him that overcometh will I make a pillar in the temple of my God, and he shall go no more out: and I will write upon him the name of my God, which is new Jerusalem, which cometh down out of heaven from my God: and I will write upon him my new name.*

Every pillar is essential to hold up the roof of a marble or stone building; when any one pillar is removed the building will collapse. Every believer is like a pillar in the building that makes up the bride of Christ and each is necessary for making up the completed body of Christ. There will never be a time when any Christian will be removed from this body of Christ.

When a child of God enters Heaven, at the time of their death, they will be identified as belonging to God and a citizen of our new home called the New Jerusalem. In chapter 22:4 it states that His name shall be in their foreheads and worn as an emblem where all can see that we belong to God and have a dwelling place in the Holy City located in Heaven. A blessed truth is found in chapter 21:2. "And I John saw the holy city, new Jerusalem, coming down from God out of heaven, prepared as a bride adorned for her husband."

Jesus said that He will write Himself a new name upon us, to identify us as belonging to Him. Perhaps this name will express His love for us or perhaps something He finds precious about us, as His Bride.

13. *He that hath an ear, let him hear what the Spirit saith unto the churches.*

The Lord Jesus, once again, calls attention to the importance of the message to the church at Philadelphia and to all who read this book of the Bible.

14. *And unto the angel of the church of the Laodiceans write; These things saith the Amen, the faithful and true witness, the beginning of the creation of God;*

The Laodicean church represents the last church period of the church age. This church period started about 1900 and will continue until the rapture of the New Testament Church, to meet the Lord Jesus in the air, and forever be with our Lord. The Amen, faithful and true witness again proclaims the Deity of Jesus to be God. This same Jesus is the God of all creation including the universe and man.

15. *I know thy works, that thou art neither cold nor hot: I would thou wert cold or hot.*

Jesus knows about every church and the members of the church. The Lord Jesus not only knows about their works, but also their motive for their works. The condemnation Jesus made is severe and the Laodicean church stands to be judged. The charge is they were half-hearted in serving the Lord. The church at Laodicea was dedicated to a ritual and form of worship, without a dedicated commitment to follow the leading of the Holy Spirit.

16. *So then because thou art lukewarm, and neither cold nor hot, I will spue thee out of my mouth.*

Jesus has made it clear that Christians who, attend church for the benefit of a social status in the community, and live in sin, will be expelled as being distasteful as drinking warm water. The Lord expects all Christians to be totally committed to Him in following the will of God for their life. Romans 12:1 "I beseech you therefore, brethren, by the mercies of God, that ye present your bodies a living sacrifice, holy, acceptable unto God, which is your reasonable service."

17. *Because thou sayest, I am rich, and increased with goods, and have need of nothing; and knowest not that thou art wretched, and miserable, and poor, and blind, and naked:*

The modern world concept is that money can get everything you need and you do not need God for anything. Living a life style of luxury often encourages people to feel complacent and as a result withdraw from a dedicated worship of God. Congregations have built beautiful and comfortable church buildings and then often forget to continue dedicated worship, and ceased in their soul winning and missionary outreach. This verse describes many churches in our community and around the world.

Such churches and people to-day are satisfied with the material wealth and are destitute of any Spiritual perception about true worship of God. Those said to be blind are those who find themselves in spiritual poverty, and are not aware of their deplorable spiritual state. Being found naked is being stripped of any consciousness of the plight of the spiritual condition, of their heart and not knowing that they are rejected by the Lord Jesus.

18. *I counsel thee to buy of me gold tried in the fire, that thou mayest be rich; and white raiment, that thou mayest be clothed, and that the shame of thy nakedness do not appear; and anoint thine eyes with eye-salve, that thou mayest see.*

The Lord Jesus instructs this church, and includes people of our age, to invest in everlasting things of spiritual value. The word "counsel" indicates those who consider themselves to have everything are those who are in need, by being in spiritual poverty.

The purchasing of gold is service to God for His Glory and this would be a radical change in their thinking about proper valuable material to be laid up in Heaven. Gold tried in the fire would identify this as something pure and precious; worthy of good works that will be laid up in Heaven. The Lord taught men to lay up their treasures in Heaven and, by this, have riches that will endure forever. Those who go to Heaven will be clothed about with Heavenly garments of white. The shame of nakedness will be evident to the lost who meet Jesus at the Great White Throne, and are not clothed in the righteousness of the Son of God.

All believers will stand before the Judgment Seat of God and never be ashamed because their past record of sin has been eradicated from the Book of Life and will never condemn them. The atonement provided through the shed blood of Jesus, on the cross, makes it certain that every child of God will be properly clothed with the righteousness of the Son of God.

The Lord Jesus advises the Laodiceans to heal their eyes with the proper corrective balm so they can see what is the only way to live and please God. The proper eye-salve is to learn and obey what the Bible teaches about the life style expected of every Christian.

19. *As many as I love, I rebuke and chasten: be zealous therefore, and repent.*

The Lord loves all mankind and seeks to save all who will come to Him for Salvation by grace through faith. Believers are a special object of God's Love and the Holy Spirit will reveal to them the sins in their life, and move to call them to repent by some experience of correction.

20. *Behold, I stand at the door, and knock: if any man hear my voice, and open the door, I will come in to him, and will sup with him, and he with me.*

The urgent call to repent and be saved is the plea made by Jesus to everyone in the last days of the Laodicean age. Jesus uses an illustration about some one who may come to your home and seek entrance by knocking at the door. Jesus is today knocking on the heart of every lost person to respond to the appeal of Jesus, to permit Him to enter their soul, and save them from all their sins. Jesus invites any lost person to open their heart and invite Jesus to come into their life. Jesus promised to come into the soul of any sincere convert who will ask Jesus to be their Saviour and Lord.

To sup with the Lord Jesus is to receive into your soul the Lord Jesus to be your Saviour. The blessings of feasting together is to share with each other the blessings we have received from God. When the lost person comes to God's table of salvation they will find blessings of salvation that will satisfy every soul who hungers for the way of eternal life. Jesus will save all who come in response to the invitation to be saved.

21. *To him that overcometh wil I grant to sit with me in my throne, even as I also overcame, and am set down with my Father in his throne.*

Every sinner who wins the victory by trusting Jesus, by faith to save them, will sit with Jesus in His Throne. To sit with Jesus in His throne is to reign with Christ during the Millennium. II Timothy 2:12 "If we suffer, we shall also reign with him: If we deny him, he also will deny us:" When a groom takes a bride and goes from the wedding to his new home he has prepared for his bride. She now lives in the home, the same as the groom, and has access to every thing that belongs to the groom. When Jesus comes back to this earth and takes His bride to Heaven, we the church will share in all that belongs to the Lord Jesus.

At the time of the resurrection of Jesus from the grave He went into the third Heaven and was seated upon the throne with the Father as God Himself; Jesus was also given a name that is above every name. Philippians 2:9 "Wherefore God also hath exalted him, and given him a name which is above every name."

22. *He that hath an ear, let him hear what the Spirit saith unto the churches.*

This is the seventh time Jesus calls attention to the importance of what has been said. What the Spirit saith is the truth from God, as spoken by Jesus to the churches.

Chapter IV

Introduction: Chapter IV explains the structure of God's governmental system in Heaven. The government in Heaven is more than adequate to carry out all of the judgments found in the Seven Sealed Book discussed in chapter 5:1. All commands are issued from the throne of God, in Heaven, to the four living creatures, and then passed on to the twenty four elders, who instruct the angels to carry out the instructions from God.

1. *After this I looked, and, behold, a door was opened in heaven: and the first voice which I heard was as it were of a trumpet talking with me; which said, Come up hither, and I will shew thee things which must be hereafter.*

   After the Lord Jesus had delivered His messages, to the seven churches; The Holy Spirit invited John to look toward the dwelling place of God. The open door was an invitation to enter and behold the Throne of God. The first voice he heard speaking to him was, as it were, a trumpet. As it were a trumpet described this voice as one with great authority. The voice that spoke to John, most likely, was the person of the Lord Jesus Christ, Revelation 1:10-11. The invitation was to enter through the open door and see what would be happening on earth, during the tribulation period.

2. *And immediately I was in the spirit; and, behold, a throne was set in heaven, and one sat on the throne.*

At that very moment, without delay, the Holy Spirit took control of John. To behold the Throne was to look upon with intense excitement. The throne was set in heaven or placed in the perfect location. John saw the Lord Jesus, in His glorified body, sitting upon that throne, in the midst of heaven. Isaiah 6:1 "In the year that king Uzziah died I saw also the Lord sitting upon a throne, high and lifted up, and his train filled the temple."

3. *And he that sat was to look upon like a jasper and a sardine stone: and there was a rainbow round about the throne, in sight like unto an emerald.*

John first describes what he sees with the many different colors of light shinning from the throne in Heaven. The jasper stone has a transparent spectrum of purple representing the Holiness of God. A sardine stone is the color of red and often this speaks of the judgment of God. The rainbow with many colors represents the grace and mercy of God. The circle of the rainbow reminds us of the unending blessings of God's covenant with man. The emerald is the color of green which calls attention to His divine love for mankind.

4. *And round about the throne were four and twenty seats; and upon the seats I saw four and twenty elders sitting, clothed in white raiment; and they had on their heads crowns of gold.*

John describes what he sees, around the Throne of God, in the midst of Heaven. There was surrounding the base of the throne twenty four seats representing lesser thrones. The elders who hold a place of governmental authority are believed to be represented by the twelve heads of the tribes of Israel and twelve apostles. The elders of Israel represent were those who were under the Law and the twelve apostles represent those who are saved and living under Grace. The elders were clothed in white garments found to be worn by the saints in Heaven. The wearing of crowns signifies that they have some authority to rule over man who lived either in the Old Testament or New Testament period. A gold crown denotes regal authority to rule from their lesser throne.

5. *And out of the throne proceeded lightings and thunderings and voices: and there were seven lamps of fire burning before the throne, which were the seven Spirits of God.*

Lightings and thunder and voices describe a place of great power and authority, as seen around, and upon, the Throne in Heaven. These descriptive words are often used to describe the omnipotent power of God. The intensity of God's judgmental power is seen in this verse.

The seven lamps are the seven departments of the workings of the Holy Spirit who protect the throne of God from, any intrusion of Satan, or any of the Demons, who may seek to overthrow God. The seven spirits are the same spirits recorded in Chapter 1:4

6. *And before the throne there was a sea of glass like unto crystal: and in the midst of the throne, and round about the throne, were four beast full of eyes before and behind.*

The sea of glass would indicate a vast expanse of area, in Heaven, and glass speaks of purity and Holiness that shines forth from God and the throne. Crystal, also, represents purity and holiness found in Heaven. Around the base of the throne area are found four living creatures who were created by God. The living creatures, most likely, are of the order of cherubim. The living creatures are in the chain of command between the throne and the twenty four elders. A command would be given to each creature according to the order of God's creation assigned to them.

Full of eyes before and behind indicates the alertness of understanding, about all things, that takes place around the throne in heaven, or any thing that may approach the throne area.

7. *And the first beast was like a lion, and the second beast like a calf, and the third beast had a face as a man, and the fourth beast was like a flying eagle.*

The four living creatures are, of the order of cherubim, endowed with great power in order to carry out the will of God. Each beast is of a different order of creation and each represents four different forms of God's creation upon the earth. The beast like a lion is responsible for carrying out any orders that God may command in respect to what He may want the wild kingdom to accomplish. The second beast like a calf is the one who deals with the domesticated animals on earth. The third beast deals with man as God desires to direct their activities on the earth. The beast like a flying eagle directs all birds or fowls to carry out the will of God.

8. *And the four beasts had each of them six wings about him; and they were full of eyes within: and they rest not day and night, saying Holy, holy, holy, Lord God Almighty, which was, and is, and is to come.*

These four living creatures have six wings like the Seraphim. The four beast, also, as the Seraphim, praise God continually in Heaven

It should be concluded that the four creatures are of the same order of God's creation as that of the Seraphim. Being full of eyes indicated they are alert and discerning about all things around the Throne of God. Eyes within suggest that they are able to detect any evil that may seek to invade the area of holiness, around the throne of God. The vigilant work they perform around the throne never ceases. They never get tired of performing the duties necessary to carry out the will of God. The four beast cry Holy, Holy, Holy without ceasing and the reason is because God is worthy of this praise. Which was, and is, and is to come is the pronouncement that God is eternal; God has always existed and forever will be Deity.

9. *And when those beasts give glory and honour and thanks to him that sat on the throne, who liveth for ever and ever,*

Any time the four living creatures give forth their anthems of praise of Holy, Holy, Holy, they are worshiping God because of His glory and honor. Thanks to God is evident because of His Holy attributes and for the extending of mercy to redeem mankind from all his sins. God who lives forever is the eternal One who never changes.

10. *The four and twenty elders fall down before him that sat on the throne, and worship him that liveth for ever and ever, and cast their crowns before the throne, saying,*

The twenty four elders prostrate themselves before the throne in Heaven as evidence of their humble submission to God on His throne. It appears that the twenty four elders join together with the four living creatures in worship and praise to God and the Lord Jesus who is seated upon the throne. The twenty four elders are human beings who were redeemed by the atonement God required of them. The crowns were given to them because of their faithfulness in serving God. In Heaven the elders fully understand every thing they achieved on earth was because of the mercy and grace of God. The elders place their crown before the Lord knowing what they are, and ever thing they achieved, was because God was working through them. The elders realized they were only instruments God used to do His will.

11. *Thou art worthy, O Lord, to receive glory and honour and power: for thou hast created all things, and for thy pleasure they are and were created.*

The twenty four elders give the reason why they were worshiping before the throne of God and this is because He only is worthy of such praise. The elders deem the Lord God to be worthy of praise because of the glory which shines forth from the presence of God, as a result of His Holiness. Honor is the recognition of the exalted place of God, on His Throne, in contrast to human creatures, who have a sinful nature. The Omnipotence of God is a reason for worship. The power of God to create all things, including the universe, is an achievement beyond human comprehension. All of creation was for the purpose of glorifying the God of creation. Every human being was permitted to be born to glorify God, and every person will glorify Him, either in this life, by being born again, or when the lost will bow in worship before the Lord Jesus at the Great White Throne Judgment of God.

Philippians 2:10 "That at the name of Jesus every knee should bow, of things in heaven, and things in earth, and things under the earth; 11. And that every tongue should confess that Jesus Christ is Lord, to the glory of God the Father."

It is amazing to realize that God created man in order that He may receive joy and fellowship with human beings He has created.

Chapter V

Introduction: God holds a seven sealed book containing the plan of redemption, of the world. The scroll was rolled into a cylinder with seven segments, each sealed, in order to conceal the plan God would use to bring the world back under His control. No man was found qualified to break the seals and carry out the judgments. Jesus came forth to take the book because He was the only One who had the power to initiate the plan which will destroy Satan's hold on the earth.

In Heaven every living person, including the angels, sing in anthems of praise, to the Son of God, who volunteered to redeem the world from all evil. When the judgments of the seven sealed book is completed the Lord Jesus will set up the Millennial Kingdom on the earth.

1. *And I saw in the right hand of him that sat on the throne a book written within and on the backside, sealed with seven seals.*

    When Daniel was writing prophecy about the end times He recorded these thoughts about the understanding God had given him about the tribulation period.

    Daniel 12:8 "And I heard, but I understood not: then said I, O my Lord, what shall be the end of these things? 9. And he said, "go thy way, Daniel: for the words are closed up and sealed till the time of the end." What the Holy Spirit had revealed to Daniel was that prophecy would not be understood until near the time of the end of the church age and the rapture of the church.

God the Father is the one on the throne, holding in his right hand a scroll, known as the Book of Redemption of the world. The scroll has writing on the front side of the scroll and, also, on the back of the scroll. Each seal sets forth how God will carry out His dealings with Satan and those who follow him. The opening of each seal from the first to the last seal, in consecutive order, indicates that each judgment will follow in sequence until all of the judgments are completed.

2. *And I saw a strong angel proclaiming with a loud voice, Who is worthy to open the book, and to loose the seals thereof?*

This mighty angel is not named who made a loud proclamation. On this occasion

Gabriel could be this angel because he has been said to have qualifications that this mighty angel possesses. Proclaiming with a loud voice assures us that this announcement is extremely important and the question must be answered. The plan of redemption is adequate but a qualified person must be found to execute the plan. It is now urgent to find someone who can execute the plan,

3. *And no man in heaven, nor in earth, neither under the earth, was able to open the book, neither to look thereon.*

No man, who was now in Heaven, or still alive on the earth, was found qualified to carry out the things found written in the seven sealed book. Man is so weak because of his depraved condition that disqualified him for this momentous task

4. *And I wept much, because no man was found worthy to open and to read the book, neither to look thereon.*

John began to weep and his cry was noted by the host of heaven. The hearts desire of all Israel is to possess the land God had promised to Abraham, Isaac, and Jacob, and to dwell there in peace. The seven sealed book contains God's plan of redemption of the land of Israel and bring peace to the Mid-East forever. When John realized that no man was found worthy to carry out the Seven Sealed Judgments, and secure peace for Israel, it moved him to tears because of this disappointment.

5. *And one of the elders saith unto me, Weep not: behold, the Lion of the tribe of Juda, the Root of David, hath prevailed to open the book, and to loose the seven seals thereof.*

The Greek understanding is one out from among the elders. The twenty four elders were studied in chapter 4:4 The consensus is the Elders were human beings who represented the Old Testament period and the New Testament period. What is seen in this verse is the elder was concerned about the emotional feelings of John. The Elder was very much informed about what was taking place in Heaven, in relation to what will happen on earth, during the Tribulation Period. The Elder informs John of the heritage of Jesus and His qualifications to enforce the requirements of the Little Book. Jesus as the Lion of Judah discloses He is the conquering One and One who Reigns. The root of David affirms that Jesus is the rightful heir to the Throne of David. The throne of David will be reestablished, in Jerusalem, during the Millennial Period. The one to prevail is Jesus who overcomes all things, as God, and He, alone, was the only One qualified to open the Book. Loosing of the seals is to actively put into action the results of the Judgments found in the Seven Sealed Book.

6. *And I beheld, and, lo, in the midst of the throne and of the four beast, and in the midst of the elders, stood a Lamb as it had been slain, having seven horns and seven eyes, which are the seven Spirits of God sent forth into all the earth.*

John looked upon the throne with great admiration. In Heaven the four living creatures occupy the area immediately around the base of the throne. In Heaven the twenty-four elders have their places of rule in a circle around the throne. The Lamb is the Lord Jesus who was slain, in order, to make the sacrifice for the sins of the world. John 1:36 "And looking upon Jesus as he walked, he saith, Behold the Lamb of God."

Seven horns indicate that the Lamb of God has complete conquering power in Heaven and on Earth. Seven eyes denote complete intelligence, known as Omniscience.

The seven eyes are, also, associated with the seven Spirits of God, discussed in chapter 1:4

7. *And he came and took the book out of the right hand of him that sat upon the throne*

Jesus, the Lamb of God, came to God the Father and took the book of redemption from the right hand of God. The taking of the Seven Sealed Book was to enact the judgments recorded in the book. The receiving of the book from the Father in Heaven assured all of Heaven that God recognized that Jesus was the only one capable of carrying out the judgments upon the earth.

8. *And when he had taken the book, the four beasts and four and twenty elders fell down before the Lamb, having every one of them harps, and golden vials full of odours, which are the prayers*

When Jesus took the book this set the stage for the final end of Satan and all of the demon that fell with him This action now assures believers that the church age will end before the tribulation period starts and finally the Millennial Kingdom will be established on the earth.

Heaven rejoices with worship and singing to the Lord Jesus who has prevailed to open the book. The four beast and twenty four elders prostrate themselves, in worship, before the Lamb of God, because He is worthy of such worship and praise.

The vials, or bowls, were made of gold to signify that these containers were precious in the sight of God. The odours were extracted from trees, in the form of gum, or spices, which gave off a pleasant fragrance, when it was burned with a hot charcoal. Inside of this delightful container and perfume were the prayers of the Saints emphasizing how precious the prayers were to God.

9. *And they sung a new song, saying, Thou art worthy to take the book, and to open the seals thereof: for thou wast slain, and hast redeemed us to God by thy blood out of every kindred, and tongue and people, and nation;*

The twenty four elders and four living creatures sing a new song. Most likely the new song is about redemption. In verse 6 John states that the Lamb had been slain to make the atonement for the sins of man. In verse 9 it is stated that Jesus was slain so that man may be redeemed. In light of this truth, we can conclude, the new song is about redemption for man and possibly about the redemption of the world. The reason Jesus is worthy to take the book is because He was the one who made the atonement on the cross, and by His shed blood man has been saved, by grace, through faith, in the blood atonement.

The scope of the blood atonement is unlimited to save any person who will, by faith, trust Jesus to save them. No person on this earth is excluded from the Mercy of God, who will forgive them, if they will repent, and trust Jesus, to save them by faith.

10. *And hast made us unto our God kings and priests: and we shall reign on the earth.*

All who are redeemed, from the earth, will rule with Christ on the earth during the millennium. The saints of God, who are the believers, are those who have been saved and will, also, minister as a priest to those who go into the millennium. Jesus will rule the whole world from Jerusalem, during the millennium, and the Christians will be the government and rule with Christ over the earth on lesser thrones.

11. *And I beheld, and I heard the voice of many angels round about the throne and the beasts and the elders: and the number of them was ten thousand times ten thousand, and thousands of thousands*;

In the center of Heaven is a throne high and lifted up and upon the throne is God the Father, Jesus the Son of God, and the Holy Spirit. Isaiah 6:1 "In the year that king Uzziah died I saw also the Lord sitting upon a throne, high and lifted up, and his train filled the temple." Around the base of this majestic throne were found four living creatures, and a circle of twenty four lesser thrones, and seated on these thrones are twenty four elders, who have the responsibility of delegating the commands of God to the angels. Surrounding this throne of God and the brilliance of the light of God's Glory, are heavenly angels, who always do the bidding of God. The number of the angels who surround the throne is about one hundred and fifty six million. The number of angels around the throne represents only a portion of the total number of angels God originally created. One third of the angels fell with Satan when they made an eternal decision to follow and believe Satan rather than God.

12. *Saying with a loud voice, Worthy is the Lamb that was slain to receive power, and riches, and wisdom, and strenght, and honour, and glory, and blessing.*

Around the Throne of God all of the Heavenly Host will praise the Lord Jesus continually who made the sacrifice, for the sins of mankind, and also, because He will carry out the judgments found in the Little Book with seven seals. The seven attributes of God are listed as a basis for their praise, unto the Son of God. Jesus is worthy of worship in recognition of His power. Jesus is Omniscient, which means, He has all power to do all things within the scope of His will. The riches of Jesus are beyond human comprehension. All things, in the universe, were created by the Trinity and belong to Jesus. The wisdom of this divine quality is possible, since Jesus knows all things that are true and just and holy. The strength of Jesus is evident, by His power and being able, to subdue all things and bringing all things under His control.. The honor of praise to Jesus is expected, because of His exalted place at the right hand of the Father. The glory is the radiance of purity that shines forth from Jesus, who is Holy and pure in all of His attributes. Blessing Jesus in praise is a result of His name which was given to Him above every name. Philippians 2:9 "Wherefore God also hath highly exalted him, and given him a name which is above every name:"

13. *And every creature which is in heaven, and on the earth, and under the earth, and such as are in the sea, and all that are in them, heard I saying, Blessing, and honour, and glory, and power, be unto him that sitteth upon the throne, and unto the Lamb for ever and ever.*

All created creatures in heaven, and upon earth, join together in praise and adoration of the Lord Jesus. Those who have died will worship in concert with all animals on earth and the fish in the oceans. Every thing that hath breath will praise the Lord Jesus because He is worthy. The Holy attributes of Jesus are, also, the theme of adoration and praise. God the Father, God the Son, and God the Holy Spirit occupy the throne in Heaven, and together, make up the Trinity of the eternal God who never changes.

14. *And the four beasts said, Amen. And the four and twenty elders fell down and worshipped him that liveth for ever and ever.*

The four living creatures give complete approval, to all worship, and praise to God, which is taking place in heaven and on the earth. The twenty four elders are those who were redeemed from among men, and are now in heaven. The elders, cognizant of their origin, are so awed by the throne, and the God Head who sits upon the throne, and the brilliance of glory they see; moves them to fall down prostrate and worship the God of all creation

Chapter VI

Introduction: Chapter six reveals the first judgments which will come upon the earth, when the first seal is broken. The first seal broken is that of deception by Satan to persuade the nations to follow him as a world leader. The second seal brings much of the world into conflict in the Mid East. The third seal records the dreadful famine that follows the war of the second seal. The number of people who die from the ravages of war are seen by the breaking of the fourth seal. The fifth seal explains that Satan will move against the Tribulation Saints to destroy them as Christian martyrs. The results of the sixth seal will be many catastrophic events people on earth will experience.

1. *And I saw when the Lamb opened one of the seals, and I heard, as it were the noise of thunder, one of the four beasts saying Come and see.*

John now sees what the results will be when Jesus breaks the first seal of the scroll.. When the Holy Spirit breathed upon John to preface a statement with the phrase, "as it were," designated the following is to be taken symbolically. John heard a loud noise which sounded like thunder. Often thunder is used to designate something terrible and severe in judgment. Most likely the living creature which had the face of a man instructed John to follow him and see something awesome to behold.

2. *And I saw, and behold a white horse: and he that sat on him had a bow; and a crown was given unto him: and he went forth conquering, and to conquer.*

The message of the rider, of the white horse, is peace and security. The rider of the white horse will be the anti-Christ, who will first appear as a peace maker, and he will convince the ten nations that he can bring peace to the Mid East Nations. The anti-Christ holds a bow which is a symbol of power. The crown represents authority given to him, to instruct the ten nation confederation, to do what is necessary, to end conflict between Israel and her border nations. The anti-Christ was able to gain military commitments from every nation north, east, and south, of Israel to unify them in an all out war to destroy Israel.

3. *And when he had opened the second seal, I heard the second beast say, Come and see.*

When Jesus the Lamb of God breaks the second seal the second living creature calls to John, to come, and see, what will be the result of the breaking of the second seal.

4. *And there went out another horse that was red: and power was given to him that sat thereon to take peace from the earth, and that they should kill one another: and there was given unto him a great sword.*

Red is the color of blood shed and destruction. The anti-Christ will persuade all the nations he advises to unite, in one great drive, and destroy Israel, and then peace will be the result. It appears that Satan believes Israel is the reason for all of the Mid-East problems. Satan who indwells a human body, as the antichrist, concludes that God is protecting Israel, and if all nations concert their attack together, they will be able to overpower God's ability to stop their drive to destroy Israel.

The great sword means that the combined forces of the anti-Christ is able to marshal on the battle field a display of force beyond what Israel could defeat.

Ezekiel 38 and 39 describe this battle which takes place near the start of the Tribulation period and should be called the first phase of the battle of Armageddon. When the Northern forces, of Russia and her satellite nations, invade Israel God intervenes and destroys five sixth of the troops who reach Megiddo. The invading nations withdraw with great losses.

5. *And when he had opened the third seal, I heard the third beast say, Come and see. And I beheld, and lo a black horse; and he that sat on him had a pair of balances in his hand.*

The black horse depicts famine which follows in a nation when the loss of their army is so great as described in Ezekiel 38 and 39. A balance held in the hand is for weighing small quantities of food. Scarcity of food will permit only a limited amount of food to be sold at one time. The loss of life is most severe in Russia and the nations that join to fight against Israel.

6. *And I heard a voice in the midst of the four beasts say, A measure of wheat for a penny, and three measures of barley for a penny; and see thou hurt not the oil and the wine.*

A penny represents a day's pay for the laborer, during New Testament times. Matthew 20:2 "And when he had agreed with the laborers for a penny a day, he sent them into his vineyard." A measure of wheat is about one and one half pints of grain. A laborer will have to use his income each day to purchase enough grain to feed him for one day. If a worker had a family it would take his wages for one day to purchase three measures of barley to feed himself and his family. The cost of cooking oil would be so expensive and scarce no one could afford to purchase the oil or wine. The oil and wine supply is not hurt because no one will buy and diminish the supply.

7. *And when he had opened the fourth seal, I heard the voice of the fourth beast say, Come and see.*

The fourth beast makes his call to John to come and see what will happen when the fourth seal judgment starts.. All four of the living creatures are active in the judgment process.

8. **And I looked, and behold a pale horse: and his name that sat on him was Death, and Hell followed with him. And power was given unto them over the fourth part of the earth, to kill with sword, and with hunger, and with death, and with the beasts of the earth.**

When John looked, and beheld, he was shocked at the number of people who died as a result of this pale horse judgment. One fourth of the world population dies as the result of the war described in Ezekiel 38 and 39 followed with death from hunger and those who were killed by wild animals.

9. *And when he had opened the fifth seal, I saw under the altar the souls of them that were slain for the word of God, and for the testimony which they held:*

God instructed Moses to construct a tabernacle on earth patterned after the one in Heaven. Moses was, also, told how to make a proper sacrifice at the Alter. Exodus 29:12 "And thou shalt take of the blood of the bullock, and put it upon the horns of the altar with thy finger, and pour all the blood beside the bottom of the alter." There is an altar in Heaven where Jesus entered when He went into Heaven after His resurrection. Hebrews 9:24 "For Christ is not entered into the holy places made with hands, which are the figures of the true; but into heaven itself, now to appear in the presence of God for us:"

The altar in Heaven is a place of security and comfort for the tribulation saints who have been martyred. The souls of these tribulation saints go to be with the Lord at the time of their execution and are placed under the Holy Altar in the

Heavenly Tabernacle. It appears that those who trust Jesus as their Lord and Saviour will be killed, by the forces of the Devil, soon after they are born again and testify of being saved.

10. *And they cried with a loud voice, saying, How long, O Lord, holy and true, dost thou not judge and avenge our blood on them that dwell on the earth?*

The martyrs remember what happened to them on the earth. The souls under the altar in Heaven call upon God to judge Satan and his followers because of the brutal treatment inflicted upon them. Avenging our blood indicated that they were butchered when they are killed.

11. *And white robes were given unto every one of them; and it was said unto them, that they should rest yet for a little season, until their fellow-servants also and their brethren, that should be killed as they were, should be fulfilled.*

White robes are the garments of Heaven, and identify those who wear them to be clothed, with the righteousness of Jesus. These martyrs were instructed to be comforted, until the end of the tribulation period, and then the anti-Christ and anti-holy spirit will be cast into the lake of fire. The reason for not ending the tribulation period now, and judging the first and second beast, is many more will be saved who have gone into the tribulation period. Mercy is still being extended to those who have not heard the plan of salvation.

12. *And I beheld when he had opened the sixth seal, and,. lo, there was a great earthquake; and the sun became black as sackcloth of hair, and the moon became as blood.*

Perhaps this earth has never experienced an earthquake of this magnitude. Joel gives some information about an earthquake during the end times. Joel 2:10 "The earth shall quake before them; the heavens shall tremble: the sun and the moon shall be dark, and the stars shall withdraw their shining:"

John uses the word, "lo", to emphasize the terrible results of the violent shaking of the earth. The extent of the shaking of the earth could be felt around the world. The eruption following the earthquake would release so much volcanic smoke and ash the atmosphere would become as dark as night.

Sackcloth of hair is a coarsely woven fabric, made from goat or camel's hair. Sackcloth was used to make some clothing, tents, sacks, or pouches to be placed over the camel to store cargo for transport. The everyday use of sackcloth would become saturated with dirt, and appear, even blacker than the dark color of the material. The volcanic ash in the atmosphere causes the light of the moon to appear red in color. The number of people who die from the quake could be in the millions.

13. *And the stars of heaven fell unto the earth, even as a fig tree casteth her untimely figs, when she is shaken of a mighty wind.*

The Lord further demonstrates His mighty power, by calling for meteors to fall through the atmosphere, and further create, within man, a state of helplessness and fear. It is very unusual for green figs to be blown off the limbs by a strong wind. In like manner, the shower of meteors of this magnitude is not normal.

14. *And the heaven departed as a scroll when it is rolled together; and every mountain and island were moved out of their places.*

The heaven departed is to separate or to be taken away. Man at this time could look up into the heavens and nothing could be seen. Two things are possible that caused the vanishing of the stellar heaven. First God may have cut off the light of the stars and nothing could be seen. Second the air pollution was so thick from the volcanoes no one could see through the dense smoke and see the heavenly bodies. What happened was literal, but to explain how God will accomplish this is unknown. The feasibility that mountains and islands being moved off their foundation is possible if the earthquake was intense enough. God can do anything that is according to His will and nothing is beyond the power of God to achieve.

15. *And the kings of the earth, and the great men, and the rich men, and the chief captains, and the mighty men, and every bondman, and every free man, hid themselves in the dens and in the rocks of the mountains;*

The listing of different ranks of men, includes every one, who was stricken by such fear they searched for some cavern or hiding place, to escape the judgments upon them. Self-preservation is the driving motive for every man.

16. *And said to the mountains and rocks, Fall on us, and hide us from the face of him that sitteth on the throne, and from the wrath of the Lamb:*

The urgent desire to be hidden from the face of God is so intense, that they had rather die than to look upon the Lord they had rejected before the Tribulation period started. The lost people know something, of the power of God and the impending judgment they will soon face.

17. *For the great day of his wrath is come; and who shall be able to stand?*

The great day of His wrath starts at the end of the dispensation of Grace and the church being caught away to meet the Lord in the air. Very soon after the rapture of the church, the day of wrath starts, and is known as the Tribulation Period. The question about who will be able to stand has an obvious answer; No one can stand.

Chapter VII

Introduction: Chapter seven is a parenthetical section, where the Holy Spirit led John, to insert some things that need to be understood, about the tribulation, before any further judgments are given. In each parenthetical chapter, John may elaborate about any subject, that needs to be explained, and may deal with any time segment of the book of Revelation.

John writes about one hundred and forty four thousand evangels, appointed to preach the gospel, during the tribulation period. John discusses, with an elder that many tribulation saints will be saved and go to heaven, perhaps, as a result of the preaching of the hundred and forty and four thousand Jews who were saved by the preaching of the two witnesses.

1. *And after these things I saw four angels standing on the four corners of the earth, holding the four winds of the earth, that the wind should not blow on the earth, nor on the sea, nor on any tree.*

    After John had written the previous chapters he saw four angels holding firmly the impending judgments to be carried out upon all the earth. The four corners have reference to the north, south, east, and west. Holding the four winds is to bring less severe punishment at this time and end the judgments for a short period of time. The calm on the sea, or tree, would mean that for a few weeks no judgments would be carried out on the sea or land area.

2. *And I saw another angel ascending from the east, having the seal of the living God:: and he cried with a loud voice to the four angels, to whom it was given to hurt the earth and the sea,*

Another angel beside the four angels John saw standing about the earth, ascends from the sun rising. The seal the angel has will be given to the hundred and forty and four thousand, called out servants of God, to protect them from being killed by the demons. This angel calls forth his message, about the sealing of God's servants, to the four angels who had the power, to destroy the earth, but instructed not to bring judgment at this time.

3. *Saying, Hurt not the earth, neither the sea, nor the trees, till we have sealed the servants of our God in their foreheads.*

The event of sealing the servants of God is so important, that every thing of judgment is put on hold, until the servants are sealed. The seal of God will be placed on their forehead where it is visible to every one including the demons and Satan's followers.

4. *And I heard the number of them which were sealed: and there were sealed an hundred and forty and four thousand of all the tribes of the children of Israel.*

There were twelve tribes who descended from Jacob and his wives. None of the twelve tribes have kept their identity. Some of the priestly families have kept their name which identifies them as the order of priests. God knows every Israelite and to what tribe they belong and twelve thousand will be chosen from each of the tribes.

The angel places God's seal on each man who is chosen from the descendants of Israel or Jacob. The Lord will choose twelve thousand men from each of the twelve tribes of Israel to make up the evangelistic body of messengers.

5. *Of the tribe of Juda were sealed twelve thousand, of the tribe of Reuben were sealed twelve thousand, Of the tribe of Gad were sealed twelve thousand.*

Judah was the son of Jacob who was born to Leah Judah stood before Joseph in Egypt and repented of his sins against him when they sold him into slavery. Reuben was the first born son of Leah and Jacob. Gad was born to Zilpah and the seventh son of Jacob. Zilpah was the maid given to Leah.

6. *Of the tribe of Aser were sealed twelve thousand. Of the tribe of Nepthalim were sealed twelve thousand. Of the tribe of Manasses were sealed twelve thousand.*

Aser was the eighth son of Jacob and born by Zilpah. Nepthalim was the sixth son of Jacob who was born by Bilhah, Rachel's maid. Manasses was the oldest son of Joseph, and he was born by his Egyptian wife.

7. *Of the tribe of Simeon were sealed twelve thousand. Of the tribe of Levi were sealed twelve thousand. Of the tribe of Issachar were sealed twelve thousand.*

Simeon was Jacob's second son, and he was born by Leah. Levi was the third son born by Leah. Issachar was born by Leah and the ninth son of Jacob.

8. *Of the tribe of Zabulon were sealed twelve thousand. Of the tribe of Joseph were sealed twelve thousand. Of the tribe of Benjamin were sealed twelve thousand.*

Zabulon was the tenth son of Jacob and was born by Leah. Joseph was the first son born by Rachel; who was the most beloved wife of Jacob. Joseph was the eleventh son of Jacob. Benjamin was the last son born to Jacob. Rachel died while giving birth to Benjamin.

9. *After this I beheld, and, lo, a great multitude, which no man could number, of all nations, and kindreds, and people, and tongues, stood before the throne, and before the Lamb, clothed with white robes, and palms in their hands;*

After the sealing of the one hundred and forty and four thousand Hebrew evangelist, John informs us about the results of their ministry. The ministry of reaching the lost people, of the tribulation period, will be world wide. The number who are in Heaven, as a result of being martyred, was so large that John could not count them. The control Satan has over the world, during the tribulation period, is so complete, he has no restraints upon him to kill all who trust Jesus to save them.

The tribulation saints are privileged, to stand before the throne in Heaven, and to behold the beauty, of the throne. The martyrs look upon the Saviour who saved them, and realize, they were so fortunate to escape the torture and death as a result of their faith in Jesus their Saviour.

The white robes are the garments of Heaven. White signifies those who wear the robes of righteous and appear as pure in the sight of God. The saints, in heaven, are clothed upon, with the righteousness of the Son of God, and they are looked upon as Holy in the presence of the heavenly angels. Holding palm branches in their hand is a sign of victory and rejoicing because, they have been redeemed and are now in heaven.

10. *And cried with a loud voice, saying, Salvation to our God which sitteth upon the throne, and unto the Lamb.*

The tribulation saints in unison call out their anthem of praise to God and the Lord Jesus for redeeming them from sins and receiving them into heaven. Salvation to God and the Lamb is, their understanding, that Salvation is a result of the mercy and the grace of God, freely extended to sinners who could not save themselves.

11. *And all the angels stood round about the throne, and about the eldlers and the four beasts, and fell before the throne on their faces, and worshipped God,.*

In the previous two verses the tribulation martyrs were praising God, and the Lamb, for their salvation and deliverance, from the tribulation persecution. The angels are around the glorious throne in heaven, with the twenty four elders, and four living creatures, worshipping God, because of, His Holy nature and the attributes of Deity. The position of worship was chosen by all to be prone on their face, as a result of, their submission and sincere worship of God.

12. *Saying, Amen: Blessing, and glory, and wisdom, and thanksgiving, and honour, and power, and might, be unto our God for ever and ever. Amen.*

The saying of amen is to bring attention to the full approval of what is being said.

The compliment of praise is because of the many wonderful attributes of God's Holy nature. God, alone, can have these attributes of Deity. The final amen is to add to the recognition of the wonders of God's Holy nature; Who is the eternal God

13. *And one of the elders answered, saying unto me, What are these which are arrayed in white robes? and whence came they?*

Often questions are asked, not to obtain information, but call attention to something already known and then call for a statement of truth. It is obvious, that the elders were fully aware as to who these tribulation saints were..

14. *And I said unto him, Sir, thou knowest, And he said to me, These are they which came out of great tribulation, and have washed their robes, and made them white in the blood of the Lamb.*

The questions of verse thirteen are now being answered, as a restatement, of an important truth, about the grace and mercy of God. It is important to inform students, of the Word of God, about those who paid such a dear price for their testimony about trusting the Lord Jesus to save them from their sins. More than the importance of their dying was the glorious truth, about having their sins forgiven by the atonement, made by the death of Jesus on the cross for the whole world. There is no other way possible, for man to be forgiven of his sins, except through the cleansing made possible by the blood atonement.

15. ***Therefore are they before the throne of God, and serve him day and night in his temple: and he that sitteth on the throne shall dwell among them.***

A summary is given about all the host of heaven and what they are doing. Every one in heaven is worshiping and serving the Lord continually. Those in heaven are involved with the temple service and worship of God. The God who sits on the throne abides, or dwells, among the hosts of heaven who recognize God is their Father and we are his children. To dwell among them carries the idea that His love will overspread the saints with protective care.

16. ***They shall hunger no more, neither thirst any more; neither shall the sun light on them, nor any heat.***

The great multitude of tribulation saints, mentioned in verse nine, is comforted in heaven. Martyrs have experienced terrible suffering, from the anti-Christ, and now death gives them their victory in heaven. They shall never hunger, any more, may indicate that they could not buy or sell anything by refusing to take the mark of the beast. Thirst could be a serious problem if you were not able to purchase water. Things that brought much discomfort will never be a problem, for the tribulation saints in heaven. During the tribulation, there will be extreme heat upon the earth, as a judgment upon the world.

Revelation 16:8-9 "And the fourth angel poured out his vial upon the sun; and power was given unto him to scorch men with fire. 9. And men were scorched with great heat, and blasphemed the name of God, which hath power over these plagues; and they repented not to give him glory."

17. *For the Lamb which is in the midst of the throne shall feed them, and shall lead them unto living fountains of waters; and God shall wipe away all tears from their eyes.*

The Lord Jesus will feed the martyrs in a blessed place of comfort. Jesus will become as a shepherd to His sheep. Jesus the shepherd will supply all the needs that satisfy and comfort. Those who profess faith, in the Son of God, will meet such resistance and persecution in the tribulation, will now experience a time when the Lord Jesus will take away all sorrow and never be brought to tears again.

Chapter VIII

Introduction: Chapter eight gives the result of the breaking of the seventh seal. A golden censer is brought forth, by an angel, which contains the prayers of Christians which have not been answered until now. A censer was a large bowl filled with fire and when cast upon the earth demonstrated the awesome power of God, who will send forth seven angels, to sound forth their judgments. This chapter records the first four trumpet judgments and the consequences that will follow.

1. *And when he had opened the seventh seal, there was silence in heave about the space of half an hour.*

   When the seventh seal is broken seven angels come forth to initiate the seven trumpet judgments. The next series of trumpet judgments is so devastating it appears to cause the host of heaven to be stricken with shock until they are moved, to remain silent in heaven, for about half an hour.

2. *And I saw the seven angels which stood before God; and to them were given seven trumpets.*

   The seven angels are standing before God leading us to believe that God Himself gave the seven trumpet judgments to the angels. A trumpet was used, in Israel, to issue commands, to the army, and to the public, as official orders of the government. Trumpet calls were accepted, as priority, above any other activity of the people. Each trumpet judgment will be sounded and nothing can cancel or change the impending results.

3. *And another angel came and stood at the altar, having a golden censer; and there was given unto him much incense, that he should offer it with the prayers of all saints upon the golden altar which was before the throne.*

Another angel than the seven angels with the seven trumpets came and stood at the altar in heaven. Some Greek text would translate, the angel stood over the altar. The angel has in his possession a golden censer. The censer was a bowl made of gold. Gold is a precious metal associated with royalty. The golden container suggests the prayers held inside are something precious in the sight of God. Adding incense to the prayers makes the contents in the censer to be a pleasant fragrance to God. Some prayers have been made that could not be answered, until this time, in the tribulation period. Christians have prayed for God to bring judgment and destruction upon the lost while they were still alive on the earth. In this dispensation of Grace, God does not judge the lost, but reserves this judgment until the time of the tribulation period. The seven years of tribulation will be the time when great judgment will be poured out on the ungodly, who have caused terrible suffering to innocent people.

4. *And the smoke of the incense, which came with the prayers of the saints, ascended up before God out of the angel's hand.*

The time for answering the prayers of the saints has come. The angel offers to God the censer with the delight of perfume, and prayers, which have been precious to God, and have been closely guarded until this time of fulfillment. Ascending up before God is a presentation, to be acted upon, in bringing judgment upon the lost, who will not repent and trust Jesus to save them.

5. *And the angel took the censer, and filled it with fire of the altar, and cast it into the earth: and there were voices, and thunderings, and lightnings, and an earthquake.*

God gives the angel permission to enact the punishment, due to those who take the mark of the beast, and rebel at the judgments of God. Fire is taken from the brazen altar, where sin is judged. Fire is the symbol for judgment upon the inhabitants of the earth. The voices, thunderings, lightnings and an earthquake, are a manifestation of the omnipotent power of God who enacts judgments which man cannot counteract or stop.

6. *And the seven angels which had the seven trumpets prepared themselves to sound.*

The next sequence of seven judgments are now to follow God's command to execute each trumpet judgment. The seven trumpet judgments are sounded, one after the other, until all seven are completed. All the angels in heaven are eager, and always ready, to carry out every command of God who is upon His Throne located in the midst of heaven.

7. *The first angel sounded, and there followed hail and fire mingled with blood, and they were cast upon the earth: and the third part of trees was burnt up, and all green grass was burnt up.*

The first judgment of the seven trumpet judgments to fall upon the earth will be hail and fire mixed with blood. At first, there does not seem to be much physical suffering for human beings from the hail and fire. The result will be the destruction, of one third, of all living plants on the earth. Famine has been a serious problem which started as a result of the first phase, of the battle of Armageddon, recorded in Ezekiel 38 & 39. God starts dealing with man, in the tribulation period, with a generous amount of grace, but each year that passes the extent of grace diminishes. Near the middle of the tribulation period, some grace is extended, to man, by burning up only one third of all green plants. Famine will become more acute, because, one third of the plants and fruit from the trees will no longer be harvested for food.

8. *And the second angel sounded, and as it were a great mountain burning with fire was cast into the sea, and the third part of the sea became blood*;

The second trumpet judgment cast into the sea a great object, about the size of a mountain. As it were, tells us the object was not a mountain but a huge object. Burning with fire, could be the result of the great speed at which the object was traveling through space. Fire is often a symbol of severe judgment. God is again extending mercy by turning one third of the sea to blood instead of turning all the sea into blood.

9. *And the third part of the creatures which were in the sea, and had life, died; and the third part of the ships were destroyed*.

Again, the famine becomes more crucial because one third of the fish were now unavailable to feed the nations. The odor from the decaying sea creatures could be so offensive that people will become sick.

Something will happen to the ships that cause them to sink in the sea which has been turned into blood. Many lives will be lost by the sinking of the ships.

10. *And the third angel sounded, and there fell a great star from heaven, burning as it were a lamp, and it fell upon the third part of the rivers, and upon the fountains of waters;*

The third of the trumpet judgments brings suffering and death, to those who never trusted Jesus as their Lord and Saviour, and go into the tribulation period. The star that falls from heaven would be a large object which will contaminate one third of the fresh water supply. God caused this object, from space, to fall on the rivers. The fire glowing from the object would indicate this may be a meteor. The object God directed to fall, when the angel sounded the trumpet, lit up the sky as a lamp would light the darkness.

In the middle of the judgments, upon the lost, God is extending mercy, by not causing all the fresh water to be made bitter.

11. *And the name of the star is called Wormwood: and the third part of the waters became wormwood; and many men died of the waters, because they were made bitter.*

Wormwood is a bitter herb found growing in the Near East. Something bitter has been associated with judgment. Amos 5:7 "Ye who turn judgment to wormwood, and leave off righteousness in the earth," One third, of the drinking water is now made so bitter, many who drink the bitter water will die. Again, God is dealing with the ungodly with the bitter judgments, because, the wicked world will not repent and trust Jesus as their personal Saviour.

12. *And the fourth angel sounded, and the third part of the sun was smitten, and the third part of the moon, and the third part of the stars; so as the third part of them was darkened, and the day shone not for a third part of it, and the night likewise..*

It appears that this fourth angel judgment is not very severe in respect to physical suffering. The third part of the light and heat of the sun was cut off. The loss of one third of sun light, during the day, would create mental anguish and fear. The sun shining for one third less each day will create a winter condition all over the world. Later the cold climate of the world will be reversed, and the earth will become extremely hot. Revelation 16:8 "And the fourth angel poured out his vial upon the sun; and power was given unto him to scorch men with fire."

13. *And I beheld, and heard an angel flying through the midst of heaven, saying with a loud voice, Woe, woe, woe, to the inhabiters of the earth by reason of the other voices of the trumpet of the three angels, which are yet to sound.*

Between the fourth and fifth trumpet judgment, an angel flies through the atmosphere, and calls to the people on earth with loud voice. The message to the people on earth is Woe, woe, woe; the best understanding of the word "woe" is pity unto all who will have to endure the next three judgments to follow.

Chapter IX

Introduction: Three woes are pronounced upon the inhabitants of the world, in chapter 8:13. Chapter nine describes the results, of the first two woes, which means pity be unto the people of the earth who endure this punishment. The fifth angel sounded the trumpet judgment, which gives Satan permission, to release the most wicked demons out of the bottomless pit. The suffering these demons inflict is a sting like that of a scorpion. These locusts like creatures will not kill, but torment, man for five months.

The second woe is the sixth trumpet judgment. The second woe results in an army of horseman which persecutes and kills those who do not repent. Just after the middle of the tribulation period, men have become so hardened against God, that almost no one now repents and trust the Saviour to save them.

1. *And the fifth angel sounded, and I saw a star fall from heaven unto the earth: and to him was given the key of the bottomless*

The fifth angel sounds the trumpet and, the suffering that follows, is called the first woe. The star that falls from heaven, unto the earth, is Satan. Luke 10:18 "And he said unto them, I beheld Satan as lightning fall from heaven." The fall of Satan is the one who fell, in the past, and will forever remain the fallen one. The time Satan fell from heaven is unknown; although, his fall had to predate the time of the creation of Adam and Eve. Satan came to the earth; the place God had created for Lucifer, before he fell. Ezekiel 28:13. "Thou hast been in Eden the garden of God; every precious stone was thy covering, the sardius, topaz, and the diamond, the beryl, the onyx and the jasper, the sapphire, the emerald, and the carbuncle, and gold: the workmanship of thy tabrets and of thy pipes was prepared in thee in the day that thou wast created." The whole earth was a beautiful garden, prepared by God, for His arch-angle Lucifer. God did not take Eden from Lucifer when he fell; He could only fall, to the earth, because he had no where else to go.

The fifth angel gave to Satan a key which is a symbol that he has permission to open the bottomless pit. There are a great number of fallen wicked angels held in the bottomless pit because of their power, to create chaos upon the earth. Now, good people do not have to suffer because of the great power these wicked demons possess. At this time, God permits the demons to be released, upon the ungodly and to inflict the punishment they deserve. II Peter 2:4 "For if God spared not the angels that sinned, but cast them down to hell, and delivered them into chains of darkness, to be reserved unto judgment;" The only pit that could exist, where there is no bottom could be found, would be in the center of the earth, where the gravitational pull would be the same, in all directions, as if you were in space.

2. *And he opened the bottomless pit; and there arose a smoke out of the pit, as the smoke of a great furnace; and the sun and the air were darkened by reason of the smoke of the pit.*

The opening of the bottomless pit, or abyss, deep in the earth would open the mantle rock through which lava, smoke, and ash, would gush forth and fill the atmosphere with black smoke.

3. *And there came out of the smoke locusts upon the earth: and unto them was given power, as the scorpions of the earth have power.*

When Satan opened the abyss locusts came out of the pit, along with the smoke. The locusts were large insect creatures, indwelt by the most wicked demon spirits that fell with Satan, and were held in prison until the middle of the tribulation period. Jude 6 "And the angels which kept not their first estate, but left their own habitation, he hath reserved in everlasting chains under darkness unto the judgment of the great day." The power these locusts had was to sting men with the hurt of a scorpion.

4. *And it was commanded them that they should not hurt the grass of the earth, neither any green thing, neither any tree; but only those men which have not the seal of God in their foreheads.*

The locusts are demon spirits who must conform to the commands of God They have great power to sting, but they cannot exceed, what God permits them to do, in exercising their hurt on man. Normal locusts eat any green vegetation, and have no stingers to hurt man. These unusual creatures are restricted by God, not to sting His one hundred and forty and four thousand servants, who preach the gospel during the tribulation. The locusts will be intelligent creatures able to recognize a seal in the foreheads of God's servants and not attack them.

5. *And to them it was given that they should not kill them, but that they should be tormented five months: and their torment was a the torment of a scorpion, when he striketh a man.*

The sting was not lethal enough to kill. Their mission was to inflict extensive pain and suffering. The number of locusts will be so numerous man cannot escape their attacks. Swarms will be stinging a person at one time. There is no place to hide from the locusts, day or night, for five months.

6. *And in those days shall men seek death, and shall not find it; and shall desire to die, and death shall flee from them.*

The intense suffering, caused by the locusts, will be so severe that man will desire to die. The earnest desire to die will not be possible because God will not extend mercy to those who have now taken the mark of the beast.

7. *And the shapes of the locusts were like unto horses prepared unto battle; and on their heads were as it were crowns like gold, and their faces were as the faces of men.*

These locust creatures do not resemble any creature found on the earth. The locusts have protection about their body so they can not be killed, like a horse covered with armor. On their head is a crown that looks like gold. The face of the locusts looks like a human face. There is no indication in the Bible about the size of these locust creatures.

8. A*nd they had hair as the hair of women, and their teeth were as the teeth of lions.*

Upon the locust's body was a human head that looked like a man which, also, had the long hair of women. The teeth of a lion would be to hold and kill their prey. The lion's teeth would indicate a vicious creature that would attack from an ambush.

9. *And they had breastplates, as it were breastplates of iron; and the sound of their wings was as the sound of chariots of many horses running to battle.*

In the medieval period of history horses had protective covering over the vital area of their body to prevent arrows or spears from penetrating and killing them. Metal was used effectively for protective armor. The armor for the locusts will be adequate to protect them from being killed by some method man may use in an effort to kill them.

The locusts were small enough that wings could sustain them in flight. The rapid movement of the wings produced a sound like the hoof beats of many horses running at a fast gate. Chariots added to the clashing and rumbling of steel wheels rolling. Men who are exhausted because of the lack of sleep will be awakened with another wave of locusts ready to sting and hurt them.

10. *And they had tails like unto scorpions, and there were stings in their tails: and their power was to hurt men five months.*

A scorpion has a stinger, curled over its back, ready to strike any creature near by.

The exposed barb is very efficient to strike and penetrate man. Five months is a long time to endure such suffering inflicted on man.

11. *And they had a king over them, which is the angel of the bottomless pit, whose name in the Hebrew is Abaddon, but in the Greek tongue hath his name Apollyon.*

The demons that escape out of the bottomless pit have a leader who is the coordinator, for a concerted effort, to punish the whole world of mankind. This most wicked, of fallen angels, will direct all other demons, to inflict the most hurt possible, for a five month period. Abaddon means destruction and Apollyon means destroyer.

At the end of the five months brings an end, of the first woe, which means pity be unto the inhabitants of the world.

12. *One woe is past; and, behold, there come two woes more hereafter.*

The warning is that one woe of trouble is now past but two more will follow and the world can expect punishment and suffering of the degree more difficult than the first woe. This verse is like the saying, "If you think this is bad wait until you see what follows."

13. *And the sixth angel sounded, and I heard a voice from the four horns of the golden altar which is before God,*

When the angel sounded the trumpet, a voice with great authority instructed this angel to release the judgment that been held in reserve until this time. The golden altar mentioned in chapter 8:3, also, called the altar of incense, is the altar where this voice is heard. The golden altar, in Heaven, is located outside of the veil surrounding the Holy of Holies. The four horns are for decoration on each corner of the altar.

14. *Saying to the sixth angel which had the trumpet, Loose the four angels which are bound in the great river Euphrates.*

These four angels discussed in chapter 7:1 were ready to inflict death, but, Jesus ordered these four wicked angels to refrain until the one hundred and forth and four thousand servants were called to serve God. The voice from the golden altar releases these wicked angels, causing many to die, at the judgment of the army of horsemen. The four angels had been bound, and now released, indicates they are fallen angels. The area on the Euphrates River appears to be the headquarters of Satan on earth.

15. *And the four angels were loosed, which were prepared for an hour, and a day, and a month, and a year, for to slay the third part of men.*

The four angels are released to cause the death of one third of all human beings on earth. The hour, day, month, and year is not how long this judgment will last but at a given appointed day and hour this army will be released to kill one third of the population of the world.

16. *And the number of the army of the horsemen were two hundred thousand thousand: and I heard the number of them.*

The number of horsemen is two hundred million, riding on horse like creatures. Where this army comes from is not certain. To be able to call this many men into a literal cavalry would seem to be impossible. This many unusual horses, may have followed the locusts out of the bottomless pit, where the most wicked of the fallen angels were held in prison.

17. *And thus I saw the horses in the vision, and them that sat on them, having breastplates of fire, and of jacinth, and brimstone: and the heads of the horses were as the heads of lions; and out of their mouths issued fire and smoke and brimstone.*

John is seeing, all of this, in a vision about the horse and rider. The armor worn by the horsemen, and around the horses, is described by the color of the armor. The breastplates were the color of fire, which is red, jacinth is purple, brimstone is yellow. In the time of the Greek Empire polished brass shields reflected sunlight with colors described by John. The head of the horses was much like a lion's head. A most unusual activity the horses could do was to blow from their mouths, fire, and smoke, and super heated fire.

18. *By these three was the third part of men killed, by the fire, and by the smoke, and by the brimstone, which issued out of their mouths.*

God is still extending mercy since only one third of men will be killed. At the end of the tribulation period, full judgment will extend no mercy, and finally all who take the mark of the beast will be killed.

Some Bible teachers accept this ability to kill, as symbolic of modern war machines. It is better to understand this to be literal, as written by John, under the influence of the Holy Spirit. These horse like creatures will be able the run down their victims and blast out of their mouth fire, smoke and brimstone. Their assault upon man is so effective that one third of the population of the world will die.

19. *For their power is in their mouth, and in their tails: for their tails were like unto serpents, and had heads, and with them they do hurt.*

The power to kill is in their mouth but it is the serpents hanging from their tail that brings physical pain. The tail is made up of several serpents, which strike a person, as the horse runs by the individual, in pursuit to kill some one else.

20. *And the rest of the men which were not killed by these plagues yet repented not of the works of their hands, that they should not worship devils, and idols of gold, and silver, and brass, and stone, and of wood: which neither can see, nor hear, nor walk:*

About half of the world population is now dead from the previous plagues. The lost people, without Christ, know that these judgments are upon them because of their sins, yet they will not repent and trust Jesus to save them. The problem the lost have is they desire to have the material things, of this world, rather than trust Jesus to save them and then be martyred for their faith in Christ.

21. *Neither repented they of their murders, nor of their sorceries, nor of their fornication, nor of their thefts.*

The extent of the depravity of man is seen, by the conduct they exhibit, near the end of the tribulation period. They murder without any conviction that it is wrong to kill. The lack of any moral standard moves them to kill for any reason they find convenient. Witchcraft is popular today and will even become more popular during the tribulation period. Satanic worship and sorcery is often linked together, in practice, and becomes intoxicating, to those who indulge in demon worship. Another sign of moral decay is the extent of immorality, to satisfy the lust of the flesh. Stealing so a person may become rich without working is a driving force in the lives of many today and this practice will get much worse in the tribulation period.

II Timothy 3:13 "But evil men and seducers shall wax worse and worse, deceiving, and being deceived."

Chapter X

Introduction: All of chapter ten explains something that is necessary, to understand, before the other judgments are given. When a segment of explanation is discussed, it may explain, something of the past, present, or future. The Lord Jesus has in His hand the Little Book, of redemption, of the world. Jesus stands upon the sea and upon the land, declaring that the time of taking possession of all the world has arrived. John was given the little book, and instructed to eat the book, which was at first sweet but became bitter because of the increased suffering caused by the following judgments

1. *And I saw another mighty angel come down from heaven, clothed with a cloud: and a rainbow was upon his head, and his face was as it were the sun, and his feet as pillars of fire*:

    The Lord Jesus is the mighty messenger that leaves heaven and comes to the earth. Jesus is clothed with light the attire of Deity. The rainbow is, also, seen in heaven as the visible evidence of God's covenant He made with man not to destroy the earth, with a flood, like the one in the days of Noah. The presence of the rainbow, attests to man, that Jesus will forever remember His covenants He has made with man. The bright light glowing from His face is the Glory associated with Deity Acts 26:13 "At midday, O king, I saw in the way a light from heaven, above the brightness of the sun, shining round about me and them which journeyed with me.

15. And I said, Who art thou, Lord? And he said, I am Jesus whom thou persecutest."

Jesus standing is an act of taking possession, as was the case, when God told Abraham that all the land he walked upon he could claim, as a possession for his descendants. Pillars of fire assures us that this is a time of judgment.

2. *And he had in his hand a little book open: and he set his right foot upon the sea, and his left foot on the earth,*

Jesus had the seven sealed book, of redemption, of the world, in His hand. The little book was opened and Jesus was actively carrying out the plan, to redeem the world, as required when the seven seals were broken. When Jesus placed His right foot on the sea and His left foot on the earth this tells us, that enough of the judgments have been instituted, and the time of completion is near enough, to lay claim to the entire world.

3. *And cried with a loud voice, as when a lion roareth: and when he had cried, seven thunders uttered their voices,*

The lion will roar to establish his territory. Jesus makes a loud proclamation the world is now under His control. Satan and all the demons are put on notice that Jesus is quickly moving, to take back the control, of the whole world. Seven stands for absolute authority and power, of God, to carry out the rest of the judgments that are to follow. Thunder is often used to describe the omnipotent capacity of God's ability to carry out the plan of redemption of the world. When God speaks to the world it reverberates through the atmosphere with the strength and authority that causes man to tremble

4. *And when the seven thunders had uttered their voices, I was about to write: and I heard a voice from heaven saying unto me, Seal up those things which the seven thunders uttered, and write them not.*

The number seven is a number of completion, about the judgments that will be administered, and bring to an end the judgments necessary to redeem the world. The message of the voice of God had to be about further judgments, yet to come, upon man. The reason why God instructed John, not to record, the message of the seven thunders is unknown, and to speculate is not appropriate.

5. *And the angel which I saw stand upon the sea and upon the earth lifted up his hand to heaven,*

Jesus lifted His hand as a visible sign that He will confirm, by an oath, the redeeming of the world is at hand and will soon be completed.

6. *And sware by him that liveth for ever and ever, who created heaven, and the things that therein are, and the earth, and the things that herein are, and the sea, and the things which are therein, that there should be time no longer.*

It was a Jewish custom to sware by one greater than your-self, to confirm that the transaction, will be carried out with out fail. Daniel 12:7 "And I heard the man clothed in linen, which was upon the waters of the river, when he held up his right hand and his left hand unto heaven, and sware by him that liveth for ever that it shall be for a time, times, and an half; and when he shall have accomplished to scatter the power of the holy people, all these things shall be finished."

The Lord Jesus is the mighty angel, who swear an oath, in the name of God the Father. The oath is made in honor of God, who is the creator of all things in Heaven, or on the Earth.

A major emphasis about the oath is the judgments have now reached a point of completion and the fulfillment of the rest of the judgments will no longer be delayed.

7. *But in the days of the voice of the seventh angel, when he shall begin to sound, the mystery of God should be finished, as he hath declared to his servants the prophets.*

It is about time for the seventh trumpet to sound, which is the third woe.

A mystery is truth hidden, until this time, and now for the first time to be fully revealed. Some information about the power, and glory, and majesty, of Jesus had been revealed in a limited revelation to the prophets, and now a more complete understanding about revealing the attributes of Jesus the coming redeemer.

8. *And the voice which I heard from heaven spake unto me again, and said, Go and take the little book which is open in the hand of the angel which standeth upon the sea and upon the earth.*

The voice John heard, from heaven, was the seventh angel, who would soon sound the seventh trumpet. John was instructed to take the little book out of the hand of Jesus the Son of God. The little book is more accurately understood to be a scroll.

9. *And I went unto the angel, and said unto him, Give me the little book. And he said unto me, Take it, and eat it up; and it shall make thy belly bitter, but it shall be in thy mouth sweet as honey.*

John approached the Lord Jesus and requested that he take the scroll. Jesus gave John permission to take the scroll, and told him to eat the little book. Jesus informed John that the contents of the book would be sweet, to his mouth, but would be bitter to digest.

Psalm 119:103 "How sweet are thy words unto my taste! yea, sweeter than honey to my mouth!". Jeremiah 15:16 "Thy words were found, and I did eat them: and thy word was unto me the joy and rejoicing of mine heart; for I am called by thy name, O Lord God of hosts." The greatest joy and delight, to most Jews, is to know that they, as a nation, will have all the land and peace God promised to Abraham and his descendants. The title of the scroll was "Israel's Title Deed" for the land of Israel, and this title, was to John the most delightful words he could ever hear. John learned about the terrible price Israel would pay, during the Tribulation

Period, to achieve the land and peace was a bitter disappointment to him.

10. *And I took the little book out of the angel's hand, and ate it up; and it was in my mouth sweet as honey: and as soon as I had eaten it, my belly was bitter.*

The title on the scroll was sweet, because, John now had in his hand, God's plan of destroying all nations that opposed Israel's claim, to the land, God had promised to Abraham. When John looked at the judgments, Israel would be experiencing, and the destructive force of the invading armies, moved John to be grieved as something bitter in his stomach

11. *And he said unto me, Thou must prophesy again before many peoples, and nations, and tongues, and kings.*

The message already given is recorded in the Seven Sealed Book. The judgments found in the scroll are now known. There will be further prophesy, revealed to the world, by the two witnesses, and the hundred and forty four thousand evangels, who will preach the gospel to all nations. It is possible that the prophesy again, will be the writings of John, as recorded in the Book of Revelation, and will be further proclaimed until the tribulation period is concluded.

ChapterXI

Introduction: Verses one through thirteen are explaining, in a survey, what will be taking place in the first half of the tribulation period. John informs us, that the Gentiles, will have some power over Israel, during the first three and one half years of the tribulation. The two witnesses are discussed as to their ministry and what will happen to them. Verse fourteen announces the sounding of the seventh trumpet judgment, which is the third woe. The message to the world causes great anger, of nations, because of the wrath of God that follows.

1. *And there was given to me a reed like unto a rod: and the angel stood, saying, Rise, and measure the temple of God, and the altar, and them that worship therein.*

   A reed is about eleven feet long and is used to measure the length of buildings.

   The angel, {Messenger}, is the Lord Jesus Christ who, in verse three, gives power to His two witnesses. The temple of God, and the altar, must be the temple that God permits to be rebuilt in Jerusalem. It is in the rebuilt temple that Israel will once again offer their sacrifices, in unbelief, by rejecting Jesus as their Messiah. The Jews will worship therein, but will not be acceptable to God, apart from trusting Jesus as their Lord and Saviour.

2. *But the court which is without the temple leave out, and measure it not; for it is given unto the Gentiles: and the holy city shall they tread under foot forty and two months.*

The court outside the temple is the area outside of the Holy place and the Holy of Holies. To measure a building, or property, is to take over that area as belonging to the individual who purchased the property. When Israel is instructed not to measure the outer court it indicates they do not have complete control of their nation Israel. The Gentiles include all nations, and people, who are not within the Hebrew family. The nations of the world are today dictating the policy Israel must follow. In the middle of the tribulation period the Antichrist will, take over the newly constructed temple and, set himself up to be worshipped as God. II Thessalonians 2:4 "Who opposeth and exalteth himself above all that is called God, or that is worshipped; so that he as God sitteth in the temple of God, showing himself that he is God."

The forty and two months will be the last three and one half years of the tribulation period. The moment the Antichrist takes over the temple, to be worshiped as God, starts what is known as the abomination of desolation. Daniel 12:11 "And from the time that the daily sacrifice shall be taken away, and the abomination that maketh desolate set up, there shall be a thousand two hundred and ninety days."

3. *And I will give power unto my two witnesses, and they shall prophesy a thousand two hundred and threescore days, clothed in sackcloth.*

God is going to bring back to the earth two, Old Testament servants of God, to be a witness to Israel that now is the time to repent and turn unto God. Elijah will be one of the two witnesses. Malachi 4:5 "Behold, I will send you Elijah the prophet before the coming of the great and dreadful day of the Lord:" The other witness is not clearly identified in the Word of God. Some believe Moses will be the other witness, because, some of the miracles performed, during the tribulation period, are the same miracles Moses called forth in

Egypt. Enoch was, a prophet, much like Elijah in that he was taken from this earth in a supernatural exodus. Enoch was translated and did not experience death. Elijah was taken up into heaven by a whirlwind and did not die. Genesis 5:24 "And Enoch walked with God: and he was not; for God took him." II Kings 2:11 "And it came to pass, as they still went on, and talked, that, behold, there appeared a chariot of fire, and horses of fire, and parted them both asunder; and Elijah went up by a whirlwind into heaven." These two men, Elijah and Enoch are the only two men ever to leave this earth and not experience physical death. In Hebrews 9:27 "And as it is appointed unto men once to die, but after this the judgment:" The Bible states that all people are appointed a time to die. Elijah and Enoch have not yet died, but, will be brought back to be the two witnesses, and then be killed, and meet the requirement, that all men will die or be changed and receive a glorified body at the second coming of Christ, for His Church.

4. *These are the two olive trees, and the two candlesticks standing before the God of the earth.*

John is using the olive trees and lamp stands to describe the witness of Elijah and Enoch, the two prophets of God. The olive tree was a valuable source of oil for cooking and oil for the lamps. Oil represents the anointing of the Holy Spirit upon Enoch and Elijah. The anointing of the Holy Spirit is power to witness, during the difficult days, of the tribulation period. The lamp stands represent the gospel, they preach, to be the light of God, in the darkness of the lost world. It is almost certain that the two witnesses, will appear at the beginning of the tribulation, and they will be killed in the middle of the tribulation. There is good evidence that the ministry of the two witnesses, will result in the conversion of the one hundred and forty and four thousand Jews. Zechariah 4:11 "Then answered I, and said unto him, What are these two olive trees upon the right side of the candlestick and upon the left side thereof? 14. Then said he, These are the two anointed ones, that stand by the Lord of the whole earth."

5. *And if any man will hurt them, fire proceedeth out of their mouth, and devoureth their enemies: and if any man will hurt them, he must in this manner be killed.*

God will send Enoch, and Elijah, to serve Him for three and one half years and, with God's protection, no one will be able to destroy them, until their ministry is completed. The lord has a unique way for the two witnesses to protect themselves. Enoch and Elijah will be able to kill those, who seek to kill them, by blowing fire out of their mouths. It will be evident, that God has given, the two witnesses supernatural power, from above, to kill in this manner. If others attempt to hurt the two witnesses they will suffer the same injury.

6. *These have power to shut heaven, that it rain not in the days of their prophecy: and have power over waters to turn them to blood, and to smite the earth with all plagues, as often as they will.*

The two witnesses will receive great power from God, to duplicate, the miracles of Elijah and Moses. These two witnesses will cause the rain to cease for three and one half years, which is the duration of their ministry in the tribulation period. This drought will cause a famine, where many will die, for the lack of food. The effects of the drought were recorded in the days of Elijah. I Kings 17:1 "And Elijah the Tishbite, who was of the inhabitants of Gilead, said unto Ahab, As the Lord God of Israel liveth, before whom I stand, there shall not be dew nor rain these years, but according to my word."

In Egypt Moses turned the water into blood and caused many plagues, to inflict suffering, upon the Egyptians. The two witnesses will be able to turn water into blood and, also, call for the plagues to punish, the followers of the antichrist. History recorded that the plagues of Egypt was a demonstration of God's power upon Moses. When the plagues are called upon the land this will be proof that God's power is upon the two witnesses. The power to bring plagues on the land was not limited to a one time appearance, but could be duplicated, as often as they desired.

7. *And when they shall have finished their testimony, the beast that ascendeth out of the bottomless pit shall make war against them, and shall overcome them, and kill them.*

The two witnesses will be called back to earth, to proclaim the gospel of salvation, to those of the tribulation. After three and one half years their ministry is completed, and now, the Lord is ready for them to die, and claim their reward in Heaven. The two witnesses have now met the requirements of Hebrews 9:27 "And as it is appointed unto men once to die, but after this the judgment: "The wild beast that ascends out of the bottomless pit is a devil possessed creature. The bottomless pit is a place, inside the earth, and this is the same place Satan will be imprisoned for the duration of the Millennium. The beast with the power of Satan will attack the two witnesses and kill them. Up until this time, none of the demons could kill the witnesses, and the beast could not kill them if God did not permit them to be killed at this time.

8. *And their dead bodies shall lie in the street of the great city, which spiritually is called Sodom and Egypt, where also our Lord was crucified.*

The death of the two witnesses will occur in the street, of the great city, and no one will move the dead bodies lying in the street. The city where our Lord was crucified is certainly Jerusalem. The great city could be applied to Jerusalem because it was a center of trade between the East and West. The title Sodom would indicate a city of sin and rejection of the Messiah. Figuratively Egypt would indicate the world of materialism and pagan worship.

9. **And they of the people and kindreds and tongues and nations shall see their dead bodies three days and an half, and shall not suffer their dead bodies to be put in graves.**

The powerful preaching, of the two witnesses, is so condemning to those who follow the antichrist that they will celebrate by showing on television around the world, the death of these servants of God. The whole world is so captivated by, what seems to be a victory for the Devil that the dead bodies are left in the street, as an object, of what they believe is a defeat of God's preachers.

10. *And they that dwell upon the earth shall rejoice over them, and make merry, and shall send gifts one to another; because these two prophets tormented them that dwelt upon the earth.*

The rebellious souls, who have chosen to follow the Devil, will rejoice when they hear the news that these two witnesses are dead. The message of condemnation and the truth about what will happen, to the lost, is most disgusting for them to hear. The lost have three and one half days to celebrate, and give gifts to each other, in this holiday festivity. The preaching of the two witnesses, about Satan, will torment the lost who have been deceived by him and all who are deceived by him will finally be cast into Hell. The condition of the world, at the middle of the tribulation period, would permit such a celebration. The end of the tribulation, and the raging battle of Armageddon, is a condition in the world that would not support such a time of rejoicing. In light of the problems of the world, when the witnesses are killed, would most certainly be in the middle of the tribulation. The conclusion is that the two witnesses had to start at the beginning of the Tribulation period and be killed in the middle of the tribulation.

11. *And after three days and an half the Spirit of life from God entered into them, and they stood upon their feet; and great fear fell upon them which saw them.*

The witnesses will serve our lord Jesus for three and one half years and the dead bodies will lie in the streets a day for each year of their preaching the gospel, in the tribulation. A possible interpretation, of the day that equals one year, is three and one half more years Jesus the Messiah will return to Mt. of Olives and Israel will see the Saviour, and be saved in one day. Zechariah 12:10 "And I will pour upon the house of David, and upon the inhabitants of Jerusalem, the spirit of grace and of supplications: and they shall look upon me whom they have pierced, and they shall mourn for him, as one shall be in bitterness for him, as one shall be in bitterness for his firstborn." Zechariah 14:4 "And his feet shall stand in that day upon the mount of Olives, which is before Jerusalem on the east,..." Romans 11:26 "And so all Israel shall be saved: as it is written, There shall come out of Sion the Deliverer, and shall turn away ungodliness from Jacob:"

God breathed the breath of life back into their dead bodied, and they stood on their feet, before all those who had rejoiced because of their death. When the ungodly saw the mighty power of God demonstrated, they feared, with a great fear. Satan's propaganda, of gaining a victory over God, now vanished and terror seized their lost soul.

12. *And they heard a great voice from heaven saying unto them, Come up hither. And they ascended up to heaven in a cloud; and their enemies beheld them.*

In verse eleven God is the source of life that returned to the witnesses. The great voice from heaven should be associated with God the Father, who commands them to leave the earth and enter into heaven. The ascension of the witnesses was of the same manner of Jesus when He returned to Heaven, from the Mt. of Olives. Acts 1:11 "Which also said, Ye men of Galilee, why stand ye gazing up into heaven? This same Jesus, which is taken up from you into heaven, shall so come in like manner as ye have seen him go into heaven." When the two witnesses were taken up into heaven, the enemies of our Lord, stood and looked into heaven, and witnessed the working of God's power, by taking the servants of God, up through the clouds.

13. *And the same hour was there a great earthquake, and the tenth part of the city fell, and in the earthquake were slain of men seven thousand: and the remnant were affrighted, and gave glory to the God of heaven.*

God further demonstrates, His mighty power, by sending a great earthquake soon after the two witnesses are taken into heaven. An earthquake creates a feeling of helplessness, when God moved to shake the earth, under the feet of those who had rejoiced at the death of the two witnesses. The city where the earthquake destroyed one tenth of the buildings was Jerusalem. Many large buildings would need to collapse for seven thousand people to be killed. The survivors, of the quake, know that God was further demonstrating His power and that He is in total control of all things in heaven and on earth. With trembling and fear the lost give glory to God by admitting that all of the things they have witnessed are the result of God's judgments upon them.

14. *The second woe is past; and, behold, the third woe cometh quickly.*

The judgments of the first two woes were very severe and brought death to many people of the tribulation. The announcement is made that the third woe is soon to be revealed with the final judgments necessary to bring an end to Satan and his followers. When the third woe starts it will bring an end quickly to the tribulation.

15. *And the seventh angel sounded; and there were great voices in heaven, saying, The kingdoms of this world are become the kingdoms of our Lord, and of his Christ; and he shall reign for ever r.*

This is the seventh and last trumpet to be sounded during the tribulation period. Another heavenly creature, perhaps Gabriel, who is the announcer of glad tidings, proclaims that this world is now taken over by the Lord Jesus. Victory has now been achieved, and it is just a matter of finishing the remaining judgments, before Jesus sets up the Millennial Kingdom and rules for a thousand years upon this earth. The throne of Jesus will be established in Jerusalem.

16. *And the four and twenty elders, which sat before God on their seats, fell upon their faces, and worshipped God,*

The twenty four elders were introduced in chapter 4:4. The elders form a circle around the base of the throne of God in heaven. The elders sit on a lesser throne and are involved in God's governmental system in heaven. The elders look upon the throne, of God, and see the Glory of Deity and are often moved to fall down on their face and worship those on the Heavenly Throne, because they are worthy of praise.

17. *Saying, We give thee thanks, O Lord God Almighty, which art and wast, and art to come; because thou hast taken to thee thy great power, and hast reigned.*

The twenty four elders represent the period of the Law and the period of Grace. We, the twenty four elders, represent all those who have, by faith, trusted the Lord to save them, by the proper atonement. All of the Elders give thanks to the Lord God for His mighty power. The Elders praise God for being the eternal and everlasting God who is omnipotent. Thanks are further offered to God, because He has now taken control of the world, and soon will set up the Millennial rule on this earth.

18. *And the nations were angry, and thy wrath is come, and the time of the dead, that they should be judged, and that thou shouldest give reward unto thy servants the prophets, and to the saints, and them that fear thy name, small and great; and shouldest destroy them which destroy the earth.*

The preaching of the hundred and forty and four thousand has informed the world about what is taking place, during the tribulation, and that the time has come for God to destroy all followers of the antichrist. The knowledge, of knowing, they have a very short time on the earth enrage those who have taken the mark of the beast.

The Bride of Christ is already in heaven and they have experienced the Judgment Seat examination, to determine their rewards. Those who are judged at the Judgment Seat include every person on earth, who by faith trusted Jesus to be their Lord and Saviour. Eventually, all who have not trusted God and the atonement, made by Jesus, will perish at the command of Jesus. Every person in the goat nations will also be destroyed at the end of the tribulation because they have sent their armies to destroy Israel

19. *And the temple of God was opened in heaven, and there was seen in his temple the ark of his testament: and there were lightnings, and voices, and thunderings, and an eartquake, and great hail.*

The temple in heaven was opened where John could see the Ark of the Covenant. Inside the ark was placed the two tables of stone upon which was inscribed the Ten Commandments. Looking at the temple and inside seeing the ark reminded John of the everlasting covenant He made with Israel, and all mankind who will be blessed because of the Saviour who would be born into this world.

Lightnings, voices, thunderings, earthquakes, and great hail are a demonstration of God's power, as seen in heaven, and by which He judges the world. God is omniscient and omnipotent and no power, in earth, or space, can overcome and defeat God and His plan of redemption of the world.

Chapter XII

Introduction: There was given to John a sign in heaven, of the nation of Israel, and the problems that the nation will have, with Satan, during the tribulation period. The Red Dragon, called Lucifer or Satan, deceived one third of the angels in heaven, to support his desire to elevate himself upon the throne of God. When Satan realizes, in the middle of the tribulation, that he will have but a short time of three and one half years on earth and now he will move with vengeance to destroy the nation; that gave birth to the Son of God. With God's help, some of the Jews will escape to Petra, and hide for the next three and one half years. Chapter twelve departs from the sequence of the judgments to explain several things that need to be understood before other judgments are released upon the world.

1. *And there appeared a great wonder in heaven; a woman clothed with the sun, and the moon under her feet, and upon her head a crown of twelve stars:*

    The sign that appears to John is the nation of Israel. Israel is considered as a woman and being clothed with the sun portrays her as a nation who gives light to the world through Jesus Christ. Isaiah 54:5 "For thy Maker is thine husband; the Lord of hosts is his name; and thy Redeemer the Holy One of Israel; The God of the whole earth shall he be called. 6. For the Lord hath called thee as a woman forsaken and grieved in spirit, and a wife of youth, when you wast refused, saith thy God." The moon under the feet of Israel suggests that this nation excels above all other nations, in their knowledge of God. Each crown represents a tribe of Israel and the blessing each of the twelve tribes will bring to the world.

2. *And she being with child cried, travailing in birth, and pained to be delivered.*

Israel was the nation God chose to give birth to the Son of God, incarnated with human flesh and dwelt among man. When Jesus was born by Mary, the nation of Israel was suffering with their unbelief and had forgotten the God who had blessed them. Israel at the time of the birth of Jesus was far from God and needed to be saved from their sins. Also, the Romans had defeated Israel and had forced them, to live under heavy Roman oppression.

3. *And there appeared another wonder in heaven; and behold a great red dragon, having seven heads and ten horns, and seven crowns upon his head.*

Another sign is seen in heaven about Satan, called the red dragon. The power and ability of the devil is seen, by the description given, in this verse. Red is the sign of danger, where cautious attention must be exercised, in dealing with this fallen angel. Seven is the number of completion, and with seven heads indicates the intelligence, he possesses, in dealing with and deceiving people. A horn is a symbol of conquering power and his ability to persuade ten nations to follow his orders to go to war with Israel and destroy them. The seven crowns tell us that his authority over the governments of the ten nations will be absolute and these nations will follow Satan's commands without questioning his motives.

4. *And his tail drew the third part of the stars of heaven, and did cast them to the earth: and the dragon stood before the woman which was ready to be delivered, for to devour her child as soon as it was born.*

Satan was a beautiful creature, and had the ability to persuade one third of the angels in heaven to agree with him, that he deserved to be elevated up on the throne of God. Isaiah 14:13 "For thou hast said in thine heart, I will ascend into heaven, I will exalt my throne above the stars of God: I will sit also upon the mount of the congregation, in the sides of the north:"

Satan was angry because he was cast out of heaven. Satan knew that some day the seed of woman would mean his defeat, and then he would be cast into hell. Satan was aware of the time, of the birth of the Son of God, and he desired to destroy the child as soon as He was born. God made sure that Jesus would not be killed before the day determined by Him for making the atonement, for the sins, of the world Matthew 2:13 "And when they were departed, behold, the angel of the Lord appeareth to Joseph in a dream, saying, Arise, and take the young child and his mother, and flee into Egypt, and be thou there until I bring word: for Herod will seek the young child to destroy him."

5. *And she brought forth a man child, who was to rule all nations with a rod of iron: and her child was caught up unto God, and to his throne.*

The time for the birth of Jesus arrived on the day, ordained, before the foundation of the world. The Lord Jesus, born with human flesh, was God who will be the king of kings, and will sit upon the throne of David, and rule the whole world during the Millennium. This ruler, is the same One, who was crucified on the cross, and was raised after three days and took His place on the throne in heaven

6. *And the woman fled into the wilderness, where she hath a place prepared of God, that they should feed her there a thousand two hundred and threescore days.*

In the middle of the tribulation period an event will take place called the abomination of desolation where Satan will go into the temple in Jerusalem and have himself proclaimed as a god to be worshiped. When the news of the abomination of desolation takes place every Hebrew who has not taken the mark of the beast must flee to the wilderness and hide for the next three and one half years or they will be killed. There is a place south of the Dead Sea called Petra where many caves are found that could be some protection for the rest of the tribulation. God will feed those people who are waiting for the coming Messiah. Matthew24:15 "When ye therefore shall see the abomination of desolation, spoken by Daniel the prophet, stand in the holy place,. [whoso readeth, let him understand:] 16. Then let them which be in Judaea flee into the mountains:"

7. *And there was war in heaven: Michael and his angels fought against the dragon; and the dragon fought and his angels,*

It must be remembered that chapter twelve is a survey chapter, and any thing may be discussed, about any event that may occur, regardless of the time it took place. The Bible is not clear as to the time this war took place in heaven. It appears, that this war could have happened before John wrote the Revelation, because, John wrote in the past tense. The important thing about this war is that Satan waged war against Michael, and his heavenly angels, and the Devil was defeated, and cast out from having a dwelling place in heaven. This may have been the time Satan waged a determined effort against Israel at the time of the birth of Christ.

8. *And prevailed not; neither was their place found any more in heaven.*

Satan, the defeated fallen angel, does not have any privilege to have a permanent dwelling in heaven. Satan has access to heaven, and even converses with God about the saints, on the earth. Job 1:6 "Now there was a day when the sons of God came to present themselves before the Lord, and Satan came also among them. 7. And the Lord said unto Satan, Whence comest thou? Then Satan answered the Lord, and said, from going to and fro in the earth, and from walking up and down in it."

9. *And the great dragon was cast out, that old serpent, called the Devil,. and Satan, which deceiveth the whole world: he was cast out into the earth, and his angels were cast out with him*

Satan is called a dragon emphasizing great in wickedness. The old serpent suggests the crooked one who strikes without warning and brings a death blow. The devil is a slanderer and accuser, Satan is the adversary, hater and accuser. The very nature of Satan is to deceive every human being and lead man to believe him in his lies. When Satan was cast out of heaven he and his fallen angels came to the earth for their dwelling place. It appears that in the original creation, of this earth, called Eden, which was a garden given to Lucifer before he fell into sin. When Satan was cast out of heaven he came to a place that was his before he fell. Ezekiel 28:13 "Thou hast, been in Eden the garden of God; every precious stone was thy covering, the sardius, topaz, and the diamond, the beryl, the onyx, and the jasper, the sapphire, the emerald, and the carbuncle, and gold; the workmanship of thy tabrets and of thy pipes was prepared in thee in the day that thou wast created."

10. *And I heard a loud voice saying in heaven, Now is come salvation, and strength, and the kingdom of our God, and the power of his Christ: for the accuser of our brethren is cast down, which accused them before our God day and night.*

This loud voice could be, the saints of God in heaven, rejoicing because they are safely in heaven and Satan has experienced another defeat. Now is come salvation is not related to the new birth, through the shed blood of Jesus, but they are now secure in heaven. The strength is that of our Lord Jesus who through His power, man has been redeemed from all their sins. The kingdom of our God is His power over all things and nothing will be lost through Satan's deceptive plan, to overthrow God. The power of Christ is found in the atonement Jesus made on the cross, which established the certain doom of Satan. The accuser of our brethren is the terminology used most often in reference to the Hebrew race, during the time of the Law. It is certain that Satan accused the Old Testament Saints as recorded in Job.1:12 "And the Lord said unto Satan, Behold, all that he hath is in thy power; only upon himself put not forth thine hand. So Satan went forth from the presence of the Lord." Satan was cast down, to the earth, and out of heaven. Cast down, in the Greek, is in the aorist tense which means this action was once and for all and for ever completed.

11. *And they overcame him by the blood of the Lamb, and by the word of their testimony; and they loved not their lives unto the death.*

The brethren who overcame were those who were accused by the Devil. The only way to gain the victory over the Devil is to trust Jesus to save you, through the atonement made, by the shed blood of Jesus who made the sacrifice, for the sins, of the world. Their testimony was made known, publicly, realizing that the ungodly would kill them. They loved not their lives is teaching us that these martyrs had rather die for their faith in Christ, than to suffer eternity in hell.

12. *Therefore rejoice, ye heavens, and ye that dwell in them. Woe to the inhabiters of the earth and of the sea! for the devil is come down unto you, having great wrath, because he knoweth that he hath but a short time.*

Those who are rejoicing are those who are already in heaven, and enjoying the blessings of being with the Saviour, who redeemed them and brought them unto Himself. Woe is the pronouncement of doom and destruction, to the people, who are lost and now living on the earth. Using the phrase, earth and sea, is a term that includes the whole world. Man is to be pitied, where ever he may live, on the earth or sea. The devil is now restricted to the earth and he knows the Word of God which informs him, that the tribulation period is seven years and at the end of the tribulation the antichrist and the false prophet will be cast into hell. Satan often tries to overthrow God's plan, to cast him into the bottomless pit for one thousand years. Every time Satan is defeated he goes into a rage of anger and directs his attacks upon mankind. When the tribulation period starts Satan knows that seven more years is all the time he has left.

13. *And when the dragon saw that he was cast unto the earth, he persecuted the woman which brought forth the man child.*

    The devil is so revengeful against God, and knowing he cannot attack God, now attacks His people the nation of Israel. God calls Israel a woman in the Old Testament days, and they have always been loved by God. At the end of the tribulation, Jesus will return to the mountain of Olives, and every person in the world shall see Him by the means of television. When Israel sees the Lord Jesus and the nail pierced hand and wound in His side they will accept Jesus as their Lord and Saviour. Zechariah 13:6 "And one shall say unto him, What are these wounds in thine hands? Then he shall answer, Those with which I was wounded in the house of my friends." The reason Satan attacks Israel is, because, the Hebrew people were the nation that gave birth to the Son of God. Jesus died on the cross, in order, that man might be saved and, finally, the casting of Satan into hell was assured by the atonement Jesus made on the cross.

14. *And to the woman were given two wings of a great eagle, that she might fly into the wilderness, into her place, where she is nourished for a time, and times, and half a time, from the face of the serpent.*

    This event takes place in the middle of the tribulation period and is called the abomination of desolation. Matthew 24:15 "When ye therefore shall see the abomination of desolation, spoken of by Daniel the prophet, stand in the holy place, {whoso readeth, let him understand:} 16. Then let them which be in Judaea flee into the mountains:" There

111

were times when God assisted the Hebrew people to flee and escape danger from their enemies by enabling them to swiftly travel to Petra and hide in the caves. God uses an illustration of lifting them up on eagles' wings so they could fly swiftly away to safety. Exodus 19:4 "Ye have seen what I did unto the Egyptians, and how I bare you on eagles' wings, and brought you unto myself." When, the abomination of desolation starts, God will assist Israel so they can escape to the caves in the mountains, south of the Dead Sea, and hide themselves from the antichrist. Those who do not flee will be forced to take the mark of the beast or be killed. Those Israelites who make it to Petra will be fed, by the Lord, for the rest of the tribulation period, lasting three and one half more years.

15. *And the serpent cast out of his mouth water as a flood after the woman, that he might cause her to be carried away of the flood.*

When Satan is notified that many of the Jews are fleeing, to escape taking the mark of the beat, he orders his army to pursue after them and destroy them. The number of Satan's army is so many that, it covers the land like a flood, as they chase after the Jews. Jeremiah 46:7 "Who is this that cometh up as a flood, whose waters are moved as the rivers? 8. Egypt riseth up like a flood, and his waters are moved like the rivers; and he saith, I will go up, and will cover the earth; I will destroy the city and the inhabitants thereof." Satan believes that his massive army can defeat those people who are assisted by God, in their effort to hide in the mountains. Many of the Jews will escape, as the Lord carries them away, as if an eagle lifts them into the sky and flies away to safety.

16. *And the earth helped the woman, and the earth opened her mouth, and swallowed up the flood which the dragon cast out of his mouth.*

Another way God assisted Israel in fleeing into the wilderness was to cause the earth to open with a great crevice between Israel and the army of Satan. The momentum of the fast moving army in pursuit of Israel will not be able to stop and the army will plunge into the earth and be killed.

17. *And the dragon was wroth with the woman, and went to make war with the remnant of her seed, which keep the commandments of God, and have the testimony of Jesus Christ.*

Satan, called the dragon, was angered to the extent of being furious with the woman, which is identified as being Israel. To make war, with the woman, is an effort to attack and destroy any descendant of the Hebrew race of people The remnant of her seed will include only a small percentage of the nation of Israel, who start into the tribulation period; Near the end of the tribulation most Jews have died for resisting Satan. Many Jews will be saved by the preaching of the one hundred and forty and four thousand evangels called out of the twelve tribes of Israel. Some will escape and hide for the last three and one half years, of the tribulation, and have an opportunity to be saved at the end of the tribulation. Those who are especially hunted down, to be killed, are those who refuse to take the mark of the beast. Any one with Jewish blood who accepts Jesus as their Saviour is marked for immediate destruction. At the very beginning of the tribulation period Satan moves to destroy God's people, who gave birth to the Son of God. Satan seeks to get revenge against God by attacking the Jews.

Chapter XIII

Introduction: Chapter thirteen is a survey chapter about the first beast and the second beast. Descriptions are given of both of these beasts and the power each possess'. This chapter discusses the events that take place during the middle of the tribulation period. The first beast issues an order, that all people must take the mark of the beast and every person must worship an image, or idol, he sets up as a symbol of his power. The second beast performs a great miracle which further deceives the people who have persuaded that the antichrist deserves to be worshiped.

1. *And I stood upon the sand of the sea, and saw a beast rise up out of the sea, having seven heads and ten horns, and upon his horns ten crowns, and upon his heads the name of blasphemy.*

   John sees a mass of humanity before him and saw the first beast, the antichrist, come up out of the mass of human beings. The antichrist will be a man who becomes Devil possessed. When the Devil enters into this human body he will become the antichrist. God permits Satan to invest his great power to this human creature and, as the Devil, will bring much suffering and death to those who follow him. The beast is the Greek word for a wild creature capable of much destruction. The seven heads indicate one who has an intellect more than adequate to deceive much of the world population. Satan with his intellect is able to persuade ten nations to follow his orders, in an effort, to destroy the nation of Israel. The horn is a symbol of conquering power to bring nations into line with his desire to be worshiped as God. The ten crowns are diadems which are a visible evidence of Satan's right and authority to rule over ten nations. The true character of the antichrist is seen by the names of blasphemy which slander the name of God who is Holy.

2. *And the beast which I saw was like unto a leopard, and his feet were as the feet of a bear, and his mouth as the mouth of a lion: and the dragon gave him power, and his seat, and great authority.*

John uses an analogy of different wild animals to describe the character of the antichrist. The leopard is swift in its pursuit of its prey and with an instinct to kill. The feet of a bear denote power and strength. The mouth of a lion brings death to its victims and tears the helpless prey to pieces, in order, to be consumed. These wild animals depict the antichrist as one who seeks, to deceive every human being, which, in the end brings spiritual death and finally to be cast into the lake of fire, called hell.

The dragon is another title for the Devil. Lucifer was an archangel before he fell into sin and was cast out of heaven. God permitted Satan to retain his power, when he fell from heaven, and with this power he was able to invest his own kind of power into the antichrist. His seat is a throne, of power, that Satan has in this world and from which he rules in the hearts of men. Great authority is a trait of Satan's personality to persuade and deceive unsuspecting naive souls.

3. *And I saw one of his heads as it were wounded to death; and his deadly wound was healed: and all the world wondered after the beast.*

During the tribulation period, there will be a confederation of ten nations, who will give their rule of government over to the antichrist. The antichrist will have such cunning ability, of deception, that he persuades ten major world powers to follow his radical ideas, for solving the world problems. Some Bible teachers have believed this to be a revived Roman Empire. The ten toes of Daniel's Image, will be a strong union of nations, held under the power of one individual called the antichrist. Daniel in describing the fourth kingdom, of his image, states that this kingdom will have strength as that of iron, also, an underlying weakness as clay. Daniel 2:42 "And as the toes of the feet were part of iron, and part of clay, so the kingdom shall be partly strong, and partly broken."

Many excellent Bible teachers have taught that the beast who was wounded to death was Nero, or some other wicked man, brought back from Hades and will become the antichrist. An example is given in Luke 16: 26 "And beside all this, between us and you there is a great gulf fixed: so that they which would pass from hence to you cannot; neither can they pass to us, that would come from hence." These verses in Luke 16:26-31 teach a principle that those who are lost and go to Hades cannot be brought back to life, and visit the earth. It is obvious that Nero, or any other person, will not be brought back to the earth during the tribulation period.

The ten horns in verse one are identified in Daniel 7:24 as ten nations or kingdoms. "And the ten horns out of this kingdom are ten kings that shall arise: and another shall arise after them; and he shall be diverse from the first, and he shall subdue three kings." In keeping with the context of verses one and two, the death blow would indicate the deadly wound was a revolt, of three nations, which made up the confederation of ten nations, the antichrist had formed to defeat God's plan of redemption of the world, as recorded in the Seven Sealed Book. Daniel 7:8 "I considered the horns, and behold, there came up among them another little horn, before whom there were three of the first horns plucked up by the roots: and, behold, in his horn were eyes like the eyes of man, and a mouth speaking great things." The wound to death would be the possibility of the near collapse of the ten power structure, of nations, when three nations withdrew from the antichrist's control over their government.

The healing of the deadly wound is when the antichrist was able to direct the seven remaining nations, into a war, and defeat the three nations and force them to rejoin the confederation of ten nations. Daniel 7:24 "And the ten horns out of this kingdom are ten kings that shall arise: and another shall rise after them; and he shall be diverse from the first, and he shall subdue three kings. 25. And he shall speak great words against the most High, and shall wear out the saints of the most High, and think to change times and laws: and they shall be given into his hand until a time and times and the dividing of time." After the antichrist defeats and brings these three nations back under his control, he will have three and one half years left on the earth, which is called the great tribulation period.

After the antichrist achieved the impossible reorganization, of the ten world power confederation, he became so popular and famous, for his achievement that the world wondered or followed after the beast.

4. *And they worshipped the dragon which gave power unto the beast: and they worshipped the beast, saying, Who is like unto the beast? who is able to make war with him?*

The wicked people, living in the tribulation, are elated by the victory of the antichrist, in the reconsolidation of the ten world nations, by defeating the three nations that succeeded in their withdrawing from Satan's confederation. The lost people know, about the supernatural power, of the antichrist, which was given to him by the dragon known as Satan. The question calls attention to the miraculous ability of the antichrist. No one seems to be able to make war against the antichrist, and win against this one, who is so shrewd in tactics of war. Victory is elating to a weary people of the tribulation and when the deadly wound of reuniting his confederation was healed they found some comfort in this success of the antichrist.

5. *And there was given unto him a mouth speaking great things and blasphemies; and power was given unto him to continue forty and two months.*

The antichrist with elation and pride of self, with his victory against the rebellious nations, now boasts of his seemingly invincible power. The next expression of self confidence is his boasting, of great things he will achieve, in the future, in his effort to over throw the throne of God. The very God, the antichrist blasphemes, is the One who permits him to hold his power for three and one half more years.

6. *And he opened his mouth in blasphemy against God, to blaspheme his name, and his tabernacle, and them that dwell in heaven.*

Profanity from the antichrist heightens, not only against God, but he also degrades His Holy Name, and the place where God dwells, including all the heavenly hosts who dwell in heaven. The wicked heart of the devil is expressed through the antichrist, a human being, who is devil possessed.

7. *And it was given unto him to make war with the saints, and to overcome them: and power was given him over all kindreds, and tongues, and nations.*

Satan working through the antichrist has great power, even with the ability to wage war with the children of God. Satan is bold, and will get into conflict, with the arch angels in heaven. Satan is never victorious over heavenly angels, but, he is capable of destroying the bodies of born again believers. The extent of the antichrists outreach will be world wide, in that all nations and people and tribes will suffer death when they refuse to take the mark of the beast.

8. *And all that dwell upon the earth shall worship him, whose names are not written in the book of life of the Lamb slain from the foundation of the world.*

The majority of the people, in the middle of the tribulation period, will take the mark of the beast. A remnant of

119

people will manage to escape the dragnet of the devil and live until the end of the tribulation period. All men who take the mark of the beast will never have their name recorded in the Lamb's Book of Life, and can only look forward to death and hell. All who take the mark of the beast, will be so deceived, that they will worship the antichrist, believing that eventually the antichrist will defeat God and His people.

9. *If any man have an ear, let him hear.*
John records an admonition to pay attention to what has been said because this is very important.

10. *He that leadeth into captivity shall go into captivity: he that killeth with the sword must be killed with the sword. Here is the patience and the faith of the saints.*
At the time, of the middle, of the tribulation period will be the beginning of the most difficult time, anyone has ever endured; for those who have trusted the Lord Jesus, and refuses to take the mark of the beast. As the persecution intensifies, and becomes unbearable, some saints will move to take captive the antichrist, and end their suffering, but they will only be taken captive themselves. If any of those who have refused to take the mark of the beast, seek to kill the antichrist, they will be executed by the same weapon they may use in an effort to kill the antichrist. The power of the antichrist will be so well organized almost no one can oppose the antichrist, and escape their capture and execution. The intensity of persecution is so great it will take those of the most enduring faith to survive.

11. *And I beheld another beast coming up out of the earth; and he had two horns like a lamb, and he spake as a dragon.*
This second beast is another human being, devil possessed, and given the position of anti Holy Spirit. Coming from the earth is one who is a human being. The Greek word translated, another beast, is another of the same kind as the first beast, the antichrist. The two horns, on a lamb, are not

used in a violent manner to subdue another animal. The two symbols of power, not used in violence, may be his power to persuade the world to worship the antichrist and the dragon, known as the devil. When the second beast speaks he says the very same things uttered by the dragon and the antichrist the first beast.

12. *And he exerciseth all the power of the first beast before him, and causeth the earth and them which dwell therein to worship the first beast, whose deadly wound was healed.*

The first beast was invested with the dragon's power and, he could do all things the devil could do. The anti Holy Spirit is now granted the same power the antichrist has and complements the power structure of the unholy trinity. The work of the Holy Spirit is to honor and glorify The Father and The Son and to lead all men to worship and give glory to Them. In the same manner the anti Holy Spirit seeks to lead all people to worship the dragon and the antichrist. The lost world is so captivated by the success of the antichrist to reorganize and strengthen his ten world powers that it seems natural to worship the antichrist. The anti Holy Spirit always led man to worship the devil and believe that he will over-come God and finally win control over the earth.

13. *And he doeth great wonders, so that he maketh fire come down from heaven on the earth in the sight of men.*

God permits the second beast to do miracles so as to further deceive those who are lost, and have taken the mark of the beast, with no possible hope of ever being saved. Calling fire down from heaven is a miracle Elijah did before the prophets of Baal. I Kings 18: 38 "Then the fire of the Lord fell, and consumed the burnt sacrifice, and the wood, and the stones, and the dust, and licked up the water that was in the trench."

There were times when wicked men rebelled against God with such a hard heart that God further hardened their heart, to believe a lie, and suffer the consequences of their stupidity, of following the devil

14. *And deceiveth them that dwell on the earth by the means of those miracles which he had power to do in the sight of the beast; saying to them that dwell on the earth, that they should make an image to the beast, which had the wound by the sword, and did live.*

The second beast called, the anti Holy Spirit, performs miracles of such magnitude that it causes the whole world to wonder about his ability and power. Deception was so convincing that most of the population, of the world, believed the lie of the devil. Propaganda was believed to the extent hat the second beast persuaded the world to construct an image, in the likeness, of the first beast. The first beast achieved an almost impossible task of bringing the rebellious nations back under his total control, in their effort to destroy God, and His people Israel. The empire of the antichrist almost collapsed but he brought it back to life by his power and persuasion to believe and follow him.

15. *And he had power to give life unto the image of the beast, that the image of the beast should both speak, and cause that as many as would not worship the image of the beast should be killed.*

There is a possibility, that the image of, the beast will have the capacity of a computer to speak and search out every person who has not taken the mark of the beast. The sound of a voice will activate the image to speak the names of those who refuse to worship the antichrist.

16. *And he causeth all, both small and great, rich and poor, free and bond, to receive a mark in their right hand, or in their foreheads*:

It makes no difference who you are, in the social rank of society, you will be demanded to take the mark of the beast. No exemptions will be granted to anyone, because, the antichrist is determined to have ever living person to accept the devil as their god and master; this is a total commitment of the soul of man to be devil controlled.

It is imperative for the mark to be seen clearly when transactions of business are conducted. Most people will expose their right hand when exchanging goods, or money. If the mark is in the forehead every one can be identified as a follower of Satan immediately.

17. *And that no man might buy or sell, save he that had the mark, or the name of the beast, or the number of his name.*

The mark, of the beast, upon man, would be something like the branding of a slave. Different methods were used, to imprint some symbol that would identify the slave or even a soldier of some ruler. The antichrist will have such a strong control over the world population and this will enable him to force every one to take the mark of the beast. If a person does not have this identifying mark it would be impossible for him to purchase any thing from any one. No one would sell to someone without the mark for fear of disobedience to the antichrist's orders and penalty perhaps of death. There is no indication in the Bible about the name that might be used in the mark.

18. *Here is wisdom. Let him that hath understanding count the number of the beast: for it is the number of a man and his number is Six hundred threescore and six.*

John is saying that you may have some understanding about the mark of the beast, because, it is the number of man. When the number of 666 is taken to identify a person, who has made a covenant with the devil, this seals the destiny and doom of that soul to hell, the lake of fire.

CHAPTER XIV

Introduction: Chapter fourteen is a survey chapter where the Holy Spirit instructed John to explain events that will take place any time during the tribulation. Verses one through five describe the character of the one hundred forty and four thousand evangels who will proclaim the gospel, of judgment, during the tribulation period. In Verses six through twenty, there will be six more angels who will proclaim different messages to the people, of the tribulation. The first angel preaches the everlasting gospel and calls man to worship and glorify God. The second angel announces that the wicked city of Babylon has fallen. The third angel informs those who take the mark of the beast that they will finally be cast into Hell. The fourth angle calls forth the reapers to gather, or cut down, the armies who have invaded Israel, during the battle of Armageddon. The fifth angel is another angel from the temple in heaven who joins in the destruction of the armies who have taken Jerusalem. The sixth angel came out from the Alter in heaven and had power over fire to destroy the enemies of Israel.

1. *And I looked, and, lo, a Lamb stood on the mount Sion and with him a hundred forty and four thousand, having his Father's name written in their foreheads.*

   Looked upon is to behold, to consider, and lo is to indicate with great interest. The Lamb is the Lord Jesus who stands on mount Sion at the beginning of the millennial rule of Christ on the earth. Hebrews gives information that mount Sion is the heavenly Jerusalem. Hebrews 12:22 "But ye are come unto mount Sion, and unto the city of the living God, the heavenly Jerusalem, and to an innumerable company of angels." This could be the view of the beginning of the millennial rule and reign of Jesus on the earth, after the end of the tribulation period. Mount Sion is the name used to identify Jerusalem, at the time, when the church is with Christ and Jesus is on the Throne of David to rule the world from Jerusalem.

The one hundred forty and four thousand are those who were commissioned by God, in chapter seven, to preach the gospel to the world. The evangels were called out of the twelve tribes of Israel, and sealed from being killed, during their ministry in the tribulation. The tribulation period has ended and the servants of God are now standing with Jesus and the Church, in the establishing of Divine rule over the whole world. The Father's name in their foreheads is the seal of divine protection, granted to them, when God called them to serve Him.

2. *And I heard a voice from heaven, as the voice of many waters, and as the voice of a great thunder: and I heard the voice of harpers harping with their harps:*

John hears the voice of God in heaven and the sound is described by using things on the earth to express great power. Many waters flowing over the land is a force man cannot stop. Man is helpless to stop this manifestation of power and helpless to stop the omnipotent power of God. The sound of thunder is a power, often frightening, and man is helpless to stop thunder. The playing of harps is a sound of rejoicing and accompanying time of rejoicing when victory has been won, over Satan, and the world of sin. There will be great joy and rejoicing in the presence of a Holy God who has great power.

3. *And they sung as it were a new song before the throne, and before the four beasts, and the elders: and no man could*

learn that song but the hundred and forty and four thousand, which were redeemed from the earth.

The messengers of God are before the throne of God. The one hundred and forty and four thousand evangels take their place, in heaven, near the throne of God. Before the messengers or ministers, who preach during the tribulation, are the twenty four elders, who sit upon a lesser thrones, who rule and reign with Christ. Near the base of the throne, the four living creatures have their place of serving God by being a liaison between God and His creatures on earth. The hundred and four and twenty thousand are unique, because, they only are able to sing this song, perhaps about redemption for those who make up the tribulation saints. Being redeemed from the earth designates that they were human beings, saved by Grace through Faith, and received the seal of God to protect them from being killed by the devil's followers.

4. *These are they which were not defiled with women; for they are virgins. These are they which follow the Lamb whithersoever he goeth. These were redeemed from among men, being the first-fruits unto God and to the Lamb.*

These servants of God have not been defiled with women; the Greek word is translated not to be soiled with women. In the Old Testament and the New Testament, words are some times used about adultery, and whoremongers, and whoring from God, to designate one who has forsaken the true and living God and worshiped idol pagan gods. Exodus 34:15 'Lest thou make a covenant with the inhabitants of the land, and they go a -whoring after their gods, and do sacrifice unto their gods, and one call thee, and thou eat of his sacrifice;" Hosea 9:1 "Rejoice not, O Israel, for joy, as other people: for thou hast gone a-whoring from thy God, thou hast loved a reward upon every cornfloor."

The one hundred forty and four thousand are not virgins because, they have never been married, but, because they are spiritually pure. They never did forsake God and become defiled with the world and it's evil. The Bible does not teach that sexual relations with your wife is defiling, but, teaches the very opposite. Hebrews 13:4 "Marriage is honourable in all, and the bed undefiled; but whoremongers and adulterers God will judge." Following the Lamb verifies that these servants have remained true and faithful to God. To be redeemed from among men is to be born-again, out from among, those of sinful humanity. Those who became the first fruits, at this time, are the Hebrews who are the first ones saved, to make up the great host of tribulation saints. These servants of God are precious to God and the Lord Jesus Christ for being faithful to God during the most trying period of man's existence on the earth.

5. *And in their mouth was found no guile: for they are without fault before the throne of God.*

Verse five gives the reason why these servants are virgins is because they never lie about who they are and about the God they serve. Without fault is no blemish could ever be found in their character, and how they lived in such a hostile world.

6. *And I saw another angel fly in the midst of heaven, having the everlasting gospel to preach unto them that dwell on the earth, and to every nation, and kindred, and tongue, and people,*

This angel is another one after the seven previous angels mentioned. This eighth angel came from the center of heaven, where the throne of God is located. The everlasting gospel they preach is the same gospel of all ages and the gospel that is eternal for those who accept Jesus as their Lord and Saviour. The gospel message is worship God, because He is holy and pure; Who created all things in Heaven and on earth. The gospel, now in the tribulation, is to trust by faith in Jesus, to save you, as required of all who are saved. To every nation is stating that every human being, regardless of who they are, must be saved by faith, trusting Jesus Christ as their Lord.

7. *Saying with a loud voice, Fear God, and give glory to him; for the hour of his judgment is come: and worship him that made heaven, and earth, and the sea, and the fountains of waters.*

An angel from heaven sounds forth a warning, to the world, that time left to repent will soon be over. God is gracious to the inhabitants, of the tribulation, to give them a solemn urgent call to repent, before it is too late. The message, of the angel, is to worship and glorify God by accepting Jesus as their Lord and Saviour. God's time to judge the world is almost upon them and to delay is to be lost. The reason they are to worship God is because He created all things, in heaven, and on the earth, including the person who hears the message of the angel. All human beings are created by God and, therefore, must give an account to his Creator.

8. *And there followed another angel, saying, Babylon is fallen, is fallen, that great city, because she made all nations drink of the wine of the wrath of her fornication.*

The angel messenger, about the judgment of Babylon, is one that followed the angel recorded in verse six. Another pronouncement is given about the fall of the wicked city of Babylon. When the statement is made twice about fallen this intensifies the understanding of the word "fallen." The Greek aorist tense of fallen is the city fell at one judgment and will be final and forever be destroyed. The rebuilt city of Babylon will be established as a great commercial center, and wickedness, of all kind, will be available to all who seek worldly pleasure. To drink of the wrath is to participate in all of the sinful activities found in Babylon.

9. *And the third angel followed them, saying, with a loud voice, If any man worship the beast and his image, and receive his mark in his forehead, or in his hand,*

This is the third angel messenger recorded in chapter fourteen. The announcement of the warning, in a loud voice, is emphasizing the importance of the message from heaven.

At the time of the abomination of desolation, which will take place in the middle of the tribulation, will be the time, when the antichrist will demand all people to take the mark of the beast and worship the antichrist. The angel warns the inhabitants, of the tribulation period, not to take the mark or worship the beast or his image and if they submit to the orders, of the antichrist, they will be lost and finally be cast into hell. The dilemma man is confronted with is if I take the mark of the beast I will live, and if I refuse to take the mark, I most likely will be killed or starve very soon.

10. *The same shall drink of the wine of the wrath of God, which is poured out without mixture into the cup of his indignation; and he shall be tormented with fire and brimstone in the presence of the holy angels, and in the presence of the Lamb:*

The same ones are those who have taken the mark of the beast. To drink of the wrath of God is to partake of His judgment, because, they took the mark of the beast and worshiped his image. Without mixture is to experience the full wrath of God; just as God warned those who sell their soul to the devil. When one substance is mixed with another substance the strength of both are reduced in the purity, of the original substance. If the original judgments of God were changed, or added with other decrees, this would diminish the original judgment God had given. God's judgments will be administered, to those who take the mark of the beast, just as God has written in His Bible. The result of God's judgment is to be tormented, in the lake of fire, forever. The lost will be judged at the Great White Throne by the Lord Jesus, as the judge, assisted by the angels who will look upon the judgment of the lost.

11. *And the smoke of their torment ascendeth up for ever and ever: and they have no rest day nor night, who worship the beast and his image, and whosoever receiveth the mark of his name.*

The rising smoke is evidence of fire and torment of those who are there for eternity. The physical pain will be the same for all who are cast into hell and the mental anguish of the soul will be of different degrees, according to their evil works. There is no place that these souls, in anguish, can find comfort and relief from their torment. Those who take the mark of the beast will be cast into the lake of fire, called hell, and there is no way to avoid their final condemnation.

12. *Here is the patience of the saints: here are they that keep the commandments of God, and the faith of Jesus.*

The two previous verses give the terrible consequences of those who take the mark of the beast or worship his image. The Holy Spirit moved John to record the difficulty, the saints of God will experience, during the tribulation. The patience of the saints, during the tribulation, will be tested time and time again, about living by faith, and doing what God expects of believers. The commandments are to trust Jesus to save them even in the certainty of death for their faith. Never worship the image or take the mark of the beast.

13. *And I heard a voice from heaven saying unto me, Write, Blesses are the dead which die in the Lord from henceforth: Yea, saith the Spirit, that they may rest from their labours; and their works do follow them.*

A very important message is given, from heaven, by the Holy Spirit. John is instructed to write that death for the believer is a way of deliverance from the difficult struggle with the antichrist. Those who die as a martyr are blessed by being present with the Lord in Heaven. Never again will Christians be pursued, persecuted, and murdered by the antichrist and his followers. The only possible place of rest for tribulation saints is to be with the Lord, in Heaven.

14. *And I looked, and behold a white cloud, and upon the cloud one sat like unto the Son of man, having on his head a golden crown, and in his hand a sharp sickle.*

John will give a view of the final battle of Armageddon through verse twenty. Verses of scripture that are known as survey sections of the Bible may review any important event in the tribulation. Often, the Lord knows that an introduction to a coming event needs to be explained before further information, of the tribulation, is discussed. Again the terms are used to describe a scene, in heaven, which expresses amazement and astonishment, by writing that I looked and could not stop gazing upon a white cloud. Often, a white cloud is seen in heaven, and most likely John is looking upon the throne of God. Daniel 7:13 "I saw in the night visions, and, behold, one like the Son of man came with the clouds of heaven, and came to the Ancient of days, and they brought him near before him."

The Son of man is the Lord Jesus Christ who is wearing a golden crown. The golden crown identifies Jesus as the king of kings, who will be the judge of all men. The gold crown is a regal crown, of royalty, and the rightful ruler of heaven and earth, and all creation. In the hand of Jesus a sickle is found ready to cut down the armies of the antichrist, who have invaded the land of Israel, in the battle of Armageddon.

15. *And another angle came out of the temple, crying with a loud voice to him that sat on the cloud, thrust in thy sickle, and reap; for the time is come for thee to reap; for the harvest of the earth is ripe.*

Another angel came from the throne area in heaven. Announcing to the world a very important message, about an event, that is about to take place on the earth. The call is to thrust in, or send forth, the instrument used in cutting down the troops who are seeking to destroy Israel. A sickle is used to cut down many stalks, of grain, in a short period of time. The sickle is used as a symbol, to convey the idea, of a very quick harvest by cutting down the enemy who has marched against Israel. At the very end of the tribulation period is the time of this harvest which will bring an end to the goat nations.

The earth is ripe for harvest and the Greek would permit a translation of, was dry, or over- ripe.

16. *And he that sat on the cloud thrust in his sickle on the earth; and the earth was reaped.*

At the time of the end of the tribulation period the Lord Jesus will put forth the sickle to harvest the armies who are involved in the battle of Armageddon. All wicked troops from the goat nations will be destroyed, and none will survive, the trampling by the Lord Jesus who, alone, will destroy the army in the field of Israel. Joel 3:13 "Put ye in the sickle, for the harvest is ripe: come, get you down; for the press is full, the vats overflow; for their wickedness is great."

17. *And another angel came out of the temple which is in heaven, he also having a sharp sickle.*

This angel came from the temple in heaven as the angel in verse fifteen. This angel will have a sickle and will be involved in the harvest of the armies engaged in the battle of Armageddon.

18. *And another angel came out from the altar, which had power over fire; and cried with a loud cry to him that had the sharp sickle, saying, Thrust in thy sharp sickle, and gather the clusters of the vine of the earth; for her grapes are fully ripe.*

The altar in heaven is a sacred place where the souls of martyrs are kept, who were martyred for their faith in Christ. Revelation 6:9 "And when he had opened the fifth seal, I saw under the altar the souls of them that were slain for the word of God, and for the testimony which they held." Power over fire indicates the execution of judgment upon the wicked inhabitants of the earth. This angel calls forth a command, from God, to start the destruction of the troops who are now fighting in the city of Jerusalem. The illustration of gathering the clusters, of grapes, describes the massive destruction of millions of troops who have moved to destroy Israel. The vines of the earth are the troops who came from the north, south, and the east, and have almost over-run Israel before the Lord Jesus thrust in His sickle. The fully ripe grapes indicate the time the sickle is used, to harvest these armies, has reached the time that could no longer be delayed.

19. *And the angel thrust in his sickle into the earth, and gathered the vine of the earth, and cast it into the great winepress of the wrath of God.*

The angel responds to the command to thrust in his sickle, which is to start the process, of destroying the armies of the antichrist. This verse is giving a description, of the actual battle of Armageddon recorded in chapter nineteen. The winepress is further discussed in chapter nineteen and verse fifteen and explains what will happen during the conflict of battle. A winepress is a cavity lined with stones or a vat hewn out in stone where grapes are placed and then trampled with the feet until the grapes are crushed and the juice can be extracted. In like manner the soldiers will be trampled as if they are grapes until they are crushed in death.

20. *And the winepress was trodden without the city, and blood came out of the winepress, even unto the horse bridles, by the space of a thousand and six hundred furlongs.*

Zechariah chapter fourteen and verse two tells us that one half of the city of Jerusalem will be taken during the battle of Armageddon. The Lord Jesus will engage Himself, to trample the army, as they mass their troops for the final assault on Jerusalem. Blood will flow from the crushed bodies until blood will flow through the valley as deep up to a horse's bridles, or about three feet deep. Israel is about two hundred miles from the north to the south and, it appears, that Jesus will trample the army for the entire distance. The number of the army who will be trampled, and crushed, could be in the millions.

Chapter XV

Introduction: Chapter fifteen is a prelude to chapter sixteen, and the judgments of the third woe. John is permitted to see into heaven and behold the vast number of tribulation saints who have been martyred for their testimony of accepting Jesus as their Lord and Saviour. John also sees the temple of the tabernacle in heaven, where the seven angels appear, with the seven last plagues to be poured out upon the world. In the temple, in heaven, John sees the smoke which indicates the presence of the Holiness of God.

1. *And I saw another sign in heaven, great and marvellous, seven angels having the seven last plagues; for in them is filled up the wrath of God.*

    An angel appears in heaven, and a sign that signified something most astounding is now being revealed. The sign, or revelation, from heaven is about something that is fatal and deadly, to the world of the ungodly. Seven is the number of completion, where the seven angels now hold the seven last judgments, to complete the requirements of redeeming the world as recorded in the seven sealed book. Filled up the wrath is culminated when these seven vials are poured out upon the earth. God will proclaim that the world is now redeemed and completely brought back under His control, and is now ready to set up the millennium, with Jesus ruling this world from the reestablished throne of David in Jerusalem.

2. *And I saw as it were a sea of glass mingled with fire: and them that had gotten the victory over the beast, and over his image, and over his mark, and over the number of his name, stand on the sea of glass, having the harps of God.*

A sea of glass describes heaven and the area that surrounds the throne of God. A sea gives the impression of the area around the throne as great and level. Glass indicates purity of the area, as pure glass, is without blemish and transparent. At this time fire is a symbol of God's judgment during the tribulation. Today, the throne of God is a place of Grace and Mercy, but this will change to judgment, for the duration of the tribulation period. Again, John mentions the tribulation martyrs, who are now in heaven, and is apparent, that they are on the sea of glass, enjoying the blessings of being with the Lord. Man is the victor over all the troubles caused by the antichrist, and his mark, when they are killed by the beast himself. Standing and playing upon their harp is an indication of worship and praise to their God who has delivered them from this wicked world.

3. *And they sing the song of Moses the servant of God, and the song of the Lamb, saying, Great and marvellous are thy works, Lord God Almighty; just and true are thy ways, thou King of saints.*

They who will be singing the song of Moses are the tribulation saints, mentioned in verse two. The theme of the song of Moses is about deliverance from the bondage in Egypt and, being set free, when God delivered them on eagles wings. Exodus 15:1 "Then sang Moses and the children of Israel this song unto the Lord, and spake, saying, I will sing unto the Lord, for he hath triumphed gloriously: the horse and his rider hath he thrown into the sea." The song of the Lamb indicates this is another song the martyrs sing, which is, also, a song of deliverance from the terrible conditions of the tribulation period. The theme of the two songs is praise unto the Lord God Almighty. The Lord is to be praised because His works are great and marvelous. The great works of God could be translated mighty or exceedingly beyond human comprehension. Marvelous or wonderful are all the ways of the work of God. The Lord God Almighty designates God to be Omnipotent, with all power, to do all that is within His will to achieve.

The attributes of God's nature is Holy and as a result He is righteous. Just means God will always deal with man justly and will, if permitted to do so, deal with man mercifully if he seeks mercy, by repenting of their sins and trusting Jesus to save them. The King of saints is a God of pure love, dealing with sinful man, and placing him as a child of God, when they trust Jesus to be the King of Kings and Lord of their lives.

4. *Who shall not fear thee, O Lord, and glorify they name? for thou only art holy: for all nations shall come and worship before thee; for thy judgments are made manifest.*

The adoration to God in the songs of Moses and the Lamb continues in verse four. The question is asked who shall not fear thee. To know God in the fullness of His Glory is to fear the Lord with reverential awe. It is normal for every human being to glorify the name of the Lord Jesus when they come to understand the attributes of His majesty and holiness. The Lord is by His very nature Holy. It is impossible for any human being to ever achieve the state of Holiness. Holiness is only found in the trinity of Deity and purity of a sinless nature is associated with God as His natural attribute.

Ever human being is born for one purpose and that is to glorify God. The saints of God will fulfill this purpose when they trust Jesus as their Saviour. The lost will, also, glorify Jesus at the great White Throne Judgment, when they behold his majesty and holiness but it will be too late to be saved, although, they will see Jesus and now realize that He was due worship from all of humanity. When the Lord Jesus sits in judgment, of the lost person from His Great White Throne, it will be obvious, that He is just and the consequences a lost person receives will be evident to them that they deserve eternal Hell for rejecting the Lord Jesus; who died for them on the cross.

5. *And after that I looked, and, behold, the temple of the tabernacle of the testimony in heaven was opened*:

John was, once again, astonished at what he saw in heaven and expressed that something was noticed of such grandeur that his attention was captivated. The temple was open and John could see the Holy of Holies, inside of the tent like structure. The ark is inside the veil of the Holy of Holies and assured Israel of His faithfulness in the keeping of the Covenants He made to their forefathers.

6. *And the seven angels came out of the temple, having the seven plagues, clothed in pure and white linen, and having their breasts girded with golden girdles*.

The seven angels who come, out of the temple, have in their possession the seven last judgments contained in vials, to be poured out upon the earth. These plagues may be translated, from the Greek, to mean something of a calamity or a wound. Often heavenly garments are described as being pure white linen and the bride of Christ will be wearing white linen in heaven. White garments symbolize the purity and sinlessness of the one who wears these garments. The golden girdle is worn by the Priest and has jewels attached to enhance the beauty of the garment..

7. *And one of the four beasts gave unto the seven angels seven golden vials full of the wrath of God, who liveth for ever and ever.*

The living creature who gave the vials to the seven angels is, most likely, the beast who had the face of a man. The channel of command, from the throne to one of the living creatures and then to the angels is the function of the chain of command of God's governmental system in heaven. The Greek translation of vial is better understood to mean bowl. Full of the wrath of God are these seven vials of judgment which will bring to an end all of the judgments contained in the seven sealed book. When the seventh vial is poured out on mankind the redemption of the earth will be completed and ready for the Lord Jesus to take control and establish the millennial kingdom on the earth. Again the eternity of God is recorded in Scripture emphasizing the Deity of God.

8. *And the temple was filled with smoke from the glory of God, and from his power; and no man was able to enter into the temple, till the seven plagues of the seven angels were fulfilled.*

The evidence, of the presence of God, is the shechinah cloud that filled the temple in the wilderness. There were times when smoke filled the temple, in heaven, which radiated from the Holiness of God. Exodus 40:34. "Then a cloud covered the tent of the congregation, and the glory of the Lord filled the tabernacle. 35. And Moses was not able to enter into the tent of the congregation, because the cloud abode thereon, and the glory of the Lord filled the tabernacle." The power of God is manifested by the brilliance of the light of God's glory. John is a created creature of God, and was not able to enter the temple, in heaven, because of the glow of the fullness of God's glory that filled the temple. The awesome demonstration of the power of God compliments the certainty of the completing of the final seven judgments.

Chapter XVI

Introduction: The seven angels pour out their vials containing the seven final judgments of God. The results of these judgments are of such intensity, of destruction, that it can be rightly classified as the great tribulation period. An angel proclaims that God is righteous, in the severity of His judgments, because, followers of the antichrist had so brutally treated and slain the saints of God When the last vial is poured out there is a mighty demonstration of power by voices, and thunders, and lightnings; and a great earthquake which destroyed cities of the world.

1. *And I heard a great voice out of the temple saying to the seven angels, Go your ways, and pour out the vials of the wrath of God upon the earth.*

    The strong and loud voice of God calls out from the temple in heaven. God's final command to start the end of the judgments is now initiated and soon final victory, of God, over evil will be finalized. These seven last judgments will be upon those who have taken the mark of the beast and now God will punish them with the fullness of His wrath. When the first of the seven seals was broken there was evidence that some mercy of God was extended to the world. Every series of Judgments that followed, the severity of each judgment was noted, and less mercy was evident. Now, the last series of the vials, there is no mercy accompanying these judgments and are more destructive than any previous judgments of the seven trumpets.

2. *And the first went, and poured out his vial upon the earth; and there fell a noisome and grievous sore upon the men which had the mark of the beast, and upon them which worshipped his image.*

The judgment of the vial is poured out over the entire world and it affected all of the inhabitants, who have taken the mark of the beast. The sore that resulted from the vial is most likely the same as the boil inflicted upon the Egyptians in the time of Moses. Exodus 9:9 "And it shall become small dust in all the land of Egypt, and shall be a boil breaking forth with bains upon man, and upon beast, throughout all the land of Egypt." A noisome and grievous boil would be the degree of excruciating pain, where death would seem to be welcomed. It appears that only those who have taken or worshiped the image of the beast will be affected with the sore.

3. *And the second angel poured out his vial upon the sea; and it became as the blood of a dead man; and every living soul died in the sea.*

Recorded in chapter six and verse eight, one fourth of the earth population dies, because of the sword, and hunger, and the beasts, of the earth. In chapter eight and verse eight, some mercy is seen, because, only one third of the sea was turned into blood and one third of the sea creatures died. It is quite obvious, that the shortage of food is still a problem for the world. The second vial judgment was without mercy, because all of the seas became blood, and all sea creatures died, and further cut the available food supply, for those who have taken the mark of the beast. The sea of blood had the repugnant odor of a dead man which indicates the foul odor will cover the earth. The hunger now is grave and the odor is so obnoxious that many cannot eat for the terrible smell.

4. *And the third angel poured out his vial upon the rivers and fountains of waters; and they became blood.*

All of the fresh water is now turned into blood. Man will drink blood, cook and bathe in blood. The judgments are getting more severe as the end of the tribulation draws near. The way the water looks, tastes, and smells is so repulsive the unsaved will hate and curse God for the plight of their condition.

5. *And I heard the angel of the waters say, Thou art righteous, O Lord, which art, and wast, and shalt be, because thou hast judged thus.*

The angel, who was involved in the vial judgments of blood, is proclaiming to any critics of God, that by doing this, God is righteous and just in all of His dealings with sinful man, who has taken the mark of the beast. The Judge, who is Jesus, the eternal God, has concluded the wicked sinners and He has concluded they deserve this judgment.

6. *For they have shed the blood of saints and prophets, and thou hast given them blood to drink; for they are worthy.*

The angel gives the reason why God gave to the world blood to drink, is because, those wicked demon- possessed people have killed the saints and prophets who were God's messengers. The angel further states that this is the kind of punishment the wicked deserve.

7. *And I heard another out of the altar say, Even so, Lord God Almighty, true and righteous are thy judgments.*

During difficult and severe problems, man has a disposition to question the justice of God. The vial judgments are the most severe man has ever experienced, and knowing the mind of the wicked, in their rage against God, have a message from heaven why these judgments are being poured out upon them. The angel from the temple, in heaven, affirms the purity of God by his judgments, which are according to what they deserve, and every test is according to that which is just.

8. *And the fourth angel poured out his vial upon the sun; and power was given unto him to scorch men with fire.*

Revelation 8:12 And the fourth angel sounded, and the third part of the sun was smitten, and the third part of the moon, and the third part of the stars; so as the third part of them was darkened, and the day shone not for a third part of it, and the night likewise.

The fourth angel sounded his trumpet judgment near the middle of the tribulation period, and the result would be a mild winter condition to exist upon the earth. Now some months later, the fourth angel pours out his vial, and the result is the heat of the sun is intensified so that the heat from the sun burns man with blisters which caused great pain. The heat of the sun, which will scorch men with fire, could be second and third degree burns over the exposed parts of their body.

9. *And men were scorched with great heat, and blasphemed the name of God, which hath power over these plagues: and they repented not to give him glory.*

The determined wicked heart, of those who have taken the mark of the beast, is hardened in their heart until their only reaction, to their suffering, is to curse and get angry with God. Their disturbed mind believes, if they curse God enough, He will stop these judgments. The violent acts of man will never moved God from His will and purpose. The lost have become so hardened against God they are not capable of repenting of their sins.

10. *And the fifth angel poured out his vial upon the seat of the beast, and his kingdom was full of darkness; and they gnawed their tongues for pain,*

This vial judgment is upon the seat, or little throne, of the antichrist located upon the earth. The result was darkness filled the earth Isaiah 60:2 "For, behold, the darkness shall cover the earth, and gross darkness the people: but the Lord shall arise upon thee, and his glory shall be seen upon thee."

Total darkness, for a long period of time, has a disposition to cause man to panic and go insane because of the extreme agony. Insanity can cause people to chew their tongues with a mind so dysfunctional that a rage may occur.

11. *And blasphemed the God of heaven because of their pains and their sores, and repented not of their deeds.*

    The deranged mind, of a heart set against God, continues to anger the ungodly to defy any intrusion of God into their lives. Now, the results of previous judgments are still being added to the new problems and causing frustration and rebellion against God. There is no indication that the lost have any regret or repentance because of their hatred for God.

12. *And the sixth angel poured out his vial upon the great river Euphrates, and the water thereof was dried up, that the way of the kings of the east might be prepared.*

    The approach of the final battle of Armageddon is now drawing near. The sixth angel, under God's command, pours out his vial which causes the Euphrates River to dry up. This is one of many occasions where God assists the antichrist, to carry out his plan, to destroy Israel but in the end finds destruction to his military plans. The antichrist is planning an all out drive, to gather the armies of the East, in a determined effort to destroy Israel. One major logistical problem the antichrist encountered was to move a massive army and supplies across the Euphrates River. The dry river valley will give the antichrist an unrestricted movement of troops, from the East and their material, toward Israel without a natural barrier. Satan believes he has a definite victory, in his grasp, only to find a total defeat when Jesus destroys the army of the antichrist who has reached Jerusalem.

13. *And I saw three unclean spirits like frogs come out of the mouth of the dragon, and out of the mouth of the beast, and out of the mouth of the false prophet.*

Considering the context of the next verse, it is certain that the unclean spirits out of their mouth are false propaganda, for the purpose of deceiving the leaders of nations, to believe the lie of Satan to attack Israel. The dragon or anti-God and the first beast is the anti-Christ and the second beast is the anti- Holy Spirit; all three make up the unholy trinity.

14. *For they are the spirits of devils, working miracles, which go forth unto the kings of the earth and of the whole world, to gather them to the battle of that great day of God Almighty.*

The unholy trinity originated from the attempt of the devil to copy God's perfect structure of government in Heaven. God permits the unholy trinity to perform some supernatural miracles so that these miracles may further deceive those people who have taken the mark of the beast. The kings of the whole world are better understood, in the Greek, to be the inhabited land Satan has been able to direct into following his leadership. The persuasive propaganda of the devil is able to convince the kings of the earth, to form themselves into a confederation, under his direction, and destroy Israel. The final conflict is known as the final phase of the battle of Armageddon. The propaganda leads the governments to believe they are now ready to gain the victory, over God's people, although, they are destined for destruction, when Jesus tramples them in the vengeance of His wrath.

15. *Behold, I come as a thief. Blessed is he that watcheth, and keepeth his garments, lest he walk naked, and they see his shame*

Near the end of the tribulation period Satan will have an effective propaganda program, deceiving the world. Jesus is warning those who have survived and have not taken the mark of the beast, and that his revelation will soon come to pass and the lost world will not expect His coming. Coming like a thief is a time when no one expects the Lord to come, to the earth, in His revelation. I Thessalonians 5:2 "For yourselves know perfectly that the day of the Lord so cometh as a thief in the night. 5. Ye are all the children of light, and the children of the day: we are not of the night, nor of darkness." Paul teaches us to be alert, as Christians, and have some knowledge about the nearness of the coming of the Lord Jesus for His church. The tribulation saints are put on notice to be alert and know that Jesus will come in His revelation at the end of the tribulation. Every tribulation believer should be looking and be ready for the Lord Jesus to return and not be caught unaware. Keeping your garments is to be alert as to the time when Jesus will return. To walk naked classifies those who are unprepared and ignorant about the Lords return, at the end of the tribulation. Those who will be ashamed are those who fail to know or understand, the Scripture, about the time when Jesus will come, to judge the goat nations, and establish the Millennium.

16. *And he gathered them together into a place called in the Hebrew tongue Armageddon.*

Armageddon is made up from two Hebrew words, "Har" which means mountain, and Mageddon, a place in the Plain of Esdraelon. Many battles have taken place in this area, in the northern part of Israel. Armageddon is the name of a place that has become synonymous with many wars, and now, the name is used to identify the last great battle of nations who will invade Israel.

17. *And the seventh angel poured out his vial into the air; and there came a great voice out of the temple of heaven, from the throne, saying, It is done.*

From the throne in the midst of Heaven, God pronounces to the lost world, that the judgments found in the seven sealed book have now been completed, and the world has been redeemed, and completely under the control of God. Satan has lost his last attempt to overthrow God and now Satan and his demons have suffered a total defeat and soon will be cast into hell.

18. *And there were voices, and thunders, and lightnings; and there was a great earthquake, such as was not since men were upon the earth, so mighty an earthquake, and so great.*

John used words that in Bible days expressed the greatest demonstration of power that man has ever experienced. Fear came upon the souls of people, two thousand years ago, when an army of yelling Roman troops ran toward their city to destroy them. Thunder storms were frightening when homes were destroyed and many lost their lives. Earthquakes were also feared because of destruction and death. The Holy Spirit moved John to use words that described great power to equate the power of God Daniel 12:1 "And at that time shall Michael stand up, the great prince which standeth for the children of thy people: and there shall be a time of trouble, such as never was since there was a nation even to that same time; and at that time thy people shall be delivered, every one that shall be found written in the book."

19. *And the great city was divided into three parts, and the cities of the nations fell: and great Babylon came in remembrance before God, to give unto her the cup of the wine of the fierceness of his wrath.*

The great city of Jerusalem separated into three parts, when the earthquake shook the city, and the world. Many cities suffered so much damage that they were classified as destroyed. Babylon is at this time known as the wicked city where sin was so prominent that God destroys this city. God's remembrance of Babylon is a sure sign that God does not overlook the wickedness of man. The cup of fierceness of his wrath does not excuse the sins of Babylon and will not permit this wickedness to continue without God judging them for their sins.

20. *And every island fled away, and the mountains were not found.*

The islands found in the seas will have the foundations shaken, so violently, that the surface of the island will slip below, the water level. Individual islands and clusters of islands will not be found, when the land slips, below the surface of the water. Mountains will also be moved from their foundations and cannot be found where they were. Rocks and earth, in some instances, will be shifted across rivers, and create dams, that will flood many areas of nations. Some mountains will be toppled over against others and, millions will die, from the violent shaking of the earth.

21. *And there fill upon men a great hail out of heaven, every stone about the weight of a talent: and men blasphemed God because of the plague of the hail; for the plague thereof was exceeding great.*

The wrath, of God is now administered with the fullness of His destructive force upon the wicked. Each segment of hail weighs about one hundred pounds. Hail falling upon the earth will destroy, many of the buildings, and kill those who are not protected from the hail. The lost people, who have taken the mark of the beast, are well aware that this calamity is another judgment from God. Instead of repenting, and calling for mercy, they from their hardened and doomed heart, will curse the very God who would have saved them, earlier, if they would have called upon God for mercy and repented; but now, it is too late, because, they have sold their soul to the devil, when they took the mark of the beast.

CHAPTER XVII

Introduction: The judgments of the Seven Sealed Book are now completed. The judgments necessary to redeem the world, from Satan, and bring it back under God's control has successfully destroyed the nations, who have believed the antichrist. The next four chapters will deal with four strongholds Satan still has intact, in order, to further destroy his influence in the world.

Chapter seventeen teaches how God will deal with, and destroy, the institution of the counterfeit religious system Satan has used effectively to deceive the world. The Holy Spirit had John to name this religious system, the great whore, because they have departed from serving the true and Living God and worshiped idols of their own creation. This religious system is noted for their great wealth and power. This religious body is, also, called mystery Babylon, because, it is the same pagan system of Babylon in mystery form. The false system is cloaked about with religious symbols and terminology. This false religious system has killed about fifty million people, during the Dark Ages, who were found not to support or may have questioned the teachings of this false religious pagan system. John informs us that this false religious system is supported by great numbers of people, around the world. Near the end of the tribulation period this religious body will be completely crushed and discarded by Satan because this religious movement is also determined to have world control.

1. *And there came one of the seven angels which had the seven vials, and talked with me, saying unto me, Come hither; I*

will shew unto thee the judgment of the great whore that sitteth upon many waters:

The seventh angel poured out his vial including and earthquake that shook the world. Perhaps this angel is the one who came to John and instructed him to come to him and see the judgment of the great whore. The term great whore has been used many times to describe cities and nations that have departed from serving the true and living God and are now serving or worshiping idol gods. During the time of the Roman Empire the worship of God had become so pagan in ritual that it truly could be called the great whore. This false religious system of paganism, galvanized with Christianity, is now supported by the masses of the population of the known world in the first century of the church. Many waters describe the mass of humanity who have embraced this false worship mingled with some Christian teachings.

2. *With whom the kings of the earth have committed fornication, and the inhabitants of the earth have been made drunk with the wine of her fornication.*

Most of the rulers of Europe, in order to hold their throne, after the second century, were forced to adhere to, and support, the leaders of the pagan state religion of Rome. Committing fornication is the interacting of their nation, and people, with the pagan worship of the Roman church. To be made drunk is adopting their false religion and making it their own system of worship. To be made drunk can, also, indicate the acceptance of something false and believing it to the point of being zealous in believing and supporting that false religion. Those committing fornication are those who are implicated in spiritual adultery by those who should have known God.

3. *So he carried me away in the spirit into the wilderness: and I saw a woman sit upon a scarlet coloured beast, full of names of blasphemy, having seven heads and ten horns.*

The angel took John apart, into a desolate place, to reveal to him some things which would soon develop out side of true Christianity. The adulterous woman is the type of an abominable form of false worship. The false religion was carried, or supported, by a beast known as the antichrist. The woman, sitting on the beast, is evidence this is a denomination supported by Satan who is also the head of this church. Every name that has been applied to Satan describes a creature who seeks to curse the name of the Lord Jesus.

Chapter thirteen and verse one the antichrist is identified as the one who has seven heads, and has great knowledge, and ten horns with the power of conquest to subdue the kings who ruled ten nations.

4. *And the woman was arrayed in purple and scarlet colour, and decked with gold and precious stones and pearls, having a golden cup in her hand full of abominations and filthiness of her fornication*:

The woman is described as the apostate religious system that has fallen into an adulterous form of religion supported by Satan. The clothing, or cloak, worn by the clergy, of purple, speaks of the most costly garments of the first century. The bright red garments were, also, the garments of the wealthy Romans. Gold ornaments and golden braid were attached to the garments, to enhance their beauty, and display the wealth of the one who wears these clothes. Other precious stones were, also, a part of the display of wealth the leaders of this false religion would wear. The golden cup, or chalice, was used in a ritual that was a perverted form of worship, that could be considered, an abomination in the sight of God because, a false religion is a departure from the atonement, God gave to the world, through the shed blood of Jesus, who died on the cross. Some Bible teachers have believed this to be a display, of the wealth, of the Roman Church.

5. *And upon her forehead was a name written, MYSTERY, BABYLON THE GREAT, THE MOTHER OF HARLOTS AND ABOMINATIONS OF THE EARTH.*

The woman in verse five has, already, been identified as the great harlot, who God knows as the mother of all false religions. The origin of pagan worship is obvious at the time of their building the tower of Babylon. Genesis 11:4 "And they said, Go to, let us build us a city and a tower, whose top may reach unto heaven; and let us make us a name, lest we be scattered abroad upon the face of the whole earth." This account, in Genesis, is an attempt, by man, to aggrandize himself and make a name for him instead of worshiping God. After the tower was destroyed, by God, the people of Babylon continued to make for themselves monuments, which later became symbols, of worship to pagan gods. This form of worship which was a departure from true worship, devoted to God, is classified as harlotry by being unfaithful to the true and living God.

A mystery is something secret and hidden from the public. Rome, in the first century, had the true gospel introduced by merchants who were saved at Pentecost and in churches after Pentecost. Paul also led many officials of government to the Lord Jesus, while imprisoned in Rome. Later paganism infiltrated the church and the clergy concealed so well their false worship that a church, that had the truth, departed from the faith, and is now identified as a harlot, who is fallen and turned away, and divorced themselves from the true and living God. This church has become an abomination, in the sight of God, because, it has become the church where millions of people have been deceived and lost. The followers of Romanism have never learned about the atonement available to all who would accept Jesus as the Lord of their lives.

6. *And I saw the woman drunken with the blood of the saints, and with the blood of the martyrs of Jesus: and when I saw her, I wondered with great admiration.*

The woman is the apostate church who has become insane, like some one who is intoxicated, by killing so many innocent Christians, or those who questioned the rituals and teachings of the Catholic Church. During the thirteenth century, a Papal Court was formed, called the Inquisition, for the purpose of finding and punishing those who did not follow the teachings of the Catholic Church. The Council of Trent met from 1545 to 1563 and agreed to end many of the corrupt practices in the church. The Council of Trent, also, endorsed the Inquisition. In 1580 to 1598 the organization of the Jesuit Order, and with the military power of Philip II, of Spain, was successful in riding Spain of Protestants. Many who opposed the Catholic Church were put to death by the most cruel manner ever devised, including burning innocent families alive at the stake.

John was informed, by the Holy Spirit, that many people would die for their faith in Jesus. John wrote that he was disturbed, and appalled to learn, that any church body of fanatics could kill about fifty million innocent people because they were suspected of disagreeing with the teachings of Rome. Many who were martyred had trusted Jesus to be their Lord and Saviour.

7. *And the angel said unto me, Wherefore didst thou marvel? I will tell thee the mystery of the woman, and of the beast that carrieth her, which hath the seven heads and ten horns.*

John will explain the mystery starting in verse eight through verse eighteen. John was astonished by the message of the angel, about the woman and the beast. The beast that carried the woman is Satan who supports this false religious body. Satan is the one who has contributed to the success of idol worship, which blinds the understanding of those who are deceived. Satan's false doctrine often enslaves the individual, to the degree, that it is difficult to witness to them about the truth of salvation by grace through faith alone.

Often the Bible identifies Satan as having seven heads and ten horns; his understanding and power are noteworthy, of repeating, so man can learn of his effectiveness in leading man astray, and final doom, of being cast into hell.

8. *The beast that thou sawest was, and is not; and shall ascend out of the bottomless pit, and go into perdition: and they that dwell on the earth shall wonder, whose names were not written in the book of life from the foundation of the world, when they behold the beast that was, and is not, and yet is.*

The beast is the antichrist that ascended out of the bottomless pit and killed the two witnesses. Revelation 11:7 "And when they shall have finished their testimony, the beast that ascended out of the bottomless pit shall make war against them, and shall overcome them, and kill them." Another group to ascend out of the bottomless pit are the most wicked demons, who have been held in the bottomless pit until this time. Revelation 9:2 "And he opened the bottomless pit; and there arose a smoke out of the pit, as the smoke of a great furnace; and the sun and the air were darkened by reason of the smoke of the pit....11. And they had a king over them, which is the angel of the bottomless pit, whose name in the Hebrew tongue is "Abaddon," but in the Greek tongue hath his name "Apollyon." The third opening of the bottomless pit will release Satan, to deceive the world, after the end of the Millennial rule has ended. Revelation 20:3 "And cast him into the bottomless pit, and shut him up, and set a seal upon him, that he should deceive the nations no more, till the thousand years should be fulfilled: and after that he must be loosed a little season."

The beast that was is a person who will some day be revealed as a demon-possessed man and will be known as the antichrist. The antichrist will make himself known to the world, at the time of the middle of the tribulation period. The beast is not known before the middle of the tribulation, although, this man could be alive today and will not gain fame for himself until after the start of the tribulation period. Revelation chapter eleven, verse seven, informs us that one of the demons out of the bottomless pit enters into a man and, as a result, he becomes the antichrist. The first beast is the antichrist, and the second beast, who is the anti holy spirit, will be cast into hell at the end of the tribulation period. Revelation 19:20 "And the beast was taken, and with him the false prophet that wrought miracles before him, with which he deceived them that had received the mark of the beast, and them that worshipped his image. These both were cast alive into a lake of fire burning with brimstone."

The lost people in the tribulation period, will be deceived, and cannot understand the truth about what God is doing. Those who do not have their names in the Lamb's Book of Life are those who have never been born again. The lost will wonder, or marvel, because of the miracle working power of the antichrist. Many lost will believe that Satan will gain the victory over God and finally gain control over the earth. When they behold the beast they will see with their eyes, the performance of miracles, and be convinced the antichrist is the one to worship; God seeks those who will worship Him by faith in Spirit and Truth.

9. *And here is the mind which hath wisdom. The seven heads are seven mountains, on which the woman sitteth..*

Unregenerate man has human wisdom and born again believers have spiritual wisdom. Human wisdom is about human fallen nature, and spiritual wisdom, knows and understands things of a spiritual nature, and the ability to understand what God is saying through His Word. The mind with wisdom is able to understand more than the natural man what the seven heads represent. The Bible has already identified the woman to be the apostate, idolatrous, religion of the world, supported by great numbers of the world population, also, a system supported and carried along by Satan. The seven mountains, in light of the context of the next verse, would be the seven major kingdoms who have embraced pagan worship as their church for their state. The woman sitteth on these seven world powers, for protection, and support, for propagating their false system of worship.

10. *And there are seven kings: five are fallen, and one is, and the other is not yet come; and when he cometh, he must continue a short space.*

John records seven major world powers that will have a tremendous impact upon mankind, before the fall of world governments, at the end of the tribulation period. The five that have already existed are clearly found in world history as fallen. 1. Egypt, 2. Assyria, 3. Babylon, 4. Persia, 5. Greece. The kingdom that existed, during the time of John, was 6.Rome. The nation that is not yet come will be the 7. Revived Roman Empire. The short time for the revived empire is of a short duration, during the seven years, of the tribulation period.

11. *And the beast that was, and is not, even he is the eighth, and is of the seven, and goeth into perdition.*

The beast that was, and is not, was explained in chapter thirteen and verse three. The antichrist will gather ten world powers under his complete control during the tribulation period. Three nations will rebel and reject the antichrist's leadership. The antichrist will be able to bring these three nations back into his confederation with his cunning appeal, of persuasion, and military force. During the tribulation period the ten nations will make up one great powerful force, and out of the revived Roman Empire, the antichrist will emerge above all other leaders, and become a mighty force for Satan. The seventh is the revived Roman Empire from which the antichrist will have his power. At the end of the tribulation period the beast, or the antichrist, will be cast into the lake of fire. Revelation 19:20 "And the beast was taken, and with him the false prophet that wrought miracles before him, with which he deceived them that had received the mark of the beast, and them that worshipped his image.

These both were cast alive into the lake of fire burning with brimstone."

12. *And the ten horns which thou sawest are ten kings, which have received no kingdom as yet; but receive power as kings one hour with the beast.*

   The ten horns represent the ten major governments that will come to power at the beginning of the tribulation period. John states that these nations are not now in existence but will be formed into a confederation in the last days. There is today, the formation of the common market in Europe, which seems to be the nucleus, upon which the last world government will be established. The formation of these ten nations, who submit to the antichrist, and his power, will last but for a short time during the tribulation period.

13. *These have one mind, and shall give their power and strength unto the beast.*

   The kings of the ten nations have reached an accord to permit the antichrist to take control of their military forces and combine their strength for any purpose he may deem necessary. The kings are deceived and have no idea that the antichrist will lead them into war against Israel when they first relinquish their power to the beast.

14. *These shall make war with the Lamb, and the Lamb shall overcome them: for he is Lord of lords, and King of kings: and they that are with him are called, and chosen, and faithful.*

   When the beast gains control of the ten nations, he thinks, he has enough strength in his armies to defeat the Lamb, who is the Lord Jesus Christ. This phase of the battle of Armageddon will take place at the end of the tribulation period. Jesus will come back to the earth, with His saints, called the Revelation of Jesus, and destroy every soldier by trampling them in the vengeance of His wrath. Jesus is very God, of Very God, and being Omnipotent, no force Satan can muster could ever hope to defeat the Lord Jesus. The saints of God will be with Jesus, in His return, but they will not be needed to assist Jesus, in his conquest, of the armies, of the antichrist.

Daniel 2:47 "The king answered unto Daniel, and said, Of a truth it is, that your God is a God of gods, and a Lord of kings, and a revealer of secrets, seeing thou couldest reveal this secret."

15. *And he saith unto me, The waters which thou sawest, where the whore sitteth, are peoples, and multitudes, and nations, and tongues.*

The Holy Spirit now breathes upon John, to explain further, who supports the whore, or woman, which represents the apostate church of Rome. The waters are representative of millions of people from all nations of all languages or dialects around the world.

16. *And the ten horns which thou sawest upon the beast, these shall hate the whore, and shall make her desolate and naked, and shall eat her flesh, and burn her with fire.*

The ten horns are the ten nations the beast has gathered about him, in a confederation and upon the beast indicates, these nations were sustained and supported by the antichrist. Near the end of the tribulation period there arises a power struggle, between Satan and the apostate church, as to who will control the masses of the population of the world. The antichrist with his ten nations does not want any competition for world control, and because of this, moves against his one time false religious system, and now moves to destroy their desire for world control. The antichrist hates the whore, or apostate religious church, and makes her desolate and naked. Bereaved with sorrow and naked means, to be stripped of any influence or power over the minds and hearts of any people. To eat her flesh and burn her with fire is to annihilate and consume any influence of power the church had in the past.

17. ***For God hath put in their hearts to fulfil his will, and to agree, and give their kingdom unto the beast, until the words of God shall be fulfilled.***

It is amazing, to learn, how God is moving to bring an end to the institutions of the devil. God has all power to do any thing according to His will, although, on this occasion God uses Satan, and his followers, to achieve His purpose and goal of obliterating, every power structure of evil. God placed into their minds to destroy the harlot church system. All of the ten world powers came to the same conclusion, to do the mind of God, not knowing that this was truly the purpose and will of God. All of the goat nations, controlled by the antichrist, relinquished their military forces to wage war against Israel. The antichrist assembled all his forces in an array, for victory over Israel, and by that defeat God's purpose, not realizing the carnage awaiting them when Jesus destroys all who attempt such an attack. When God uses the forces of evil, to achieve His objectives, they will be fulfilled perfectly according to what God willed to achieve.

18. ***And the woman which thou sawest is that great city, which reigneth over the kings of the earth.***

The woman is the apostate religious system which had it origin in Babylon. The movement of civilization has moved to the West and now Rome is the city where Mystery Babylon is found and is known as a union of church and state which holds power and dominion over the kings of other nations.

Chapter XVIII

Introduction: Some Bible teachers identify the ancient city of Babylon to be the place where Satan will locate his headquarters. Today the ancient city of Babylon is in ruins. There has been some interest in restoring the ancient city, and making it a tourist center, that would attract travelers, from a round the world. During the Tribulation Period, there will be a great city of commerce constructed on the site of old Babylon. Many nations, from a round the world, will be drawn to the reconstructed city of Babylon to purchase and sell the products for a profit. The new Babylon will become a very sinful city, with all kinds of sins the lost and depraved hearts may desire. The wickedness of Babylon becomes so great, that God chooses to destroy the city with fire, and as a result Satan's political system is destroyed.

1. *And after these things I saw another angel come down from heaven, having great power; and the earth was lightened with his glory.*

    After God has destroyed Satan's counterfeit religious system, another angel comes from heaven announcing the destruction of Babylon. The angel is seen as having great power and by this identifies the angel as an archangel from the throne of God. The people on earth saw the brightness of the shechinah glory, emanating from the angel, who came from the presence of a Holy God.

2. *And he cried mightily with a strong voice, saying, Babylon the great is fallen, is fallen, and is become the habitation of devils, and the hold of every foul spirit, and a cage of every unclean and hateful bird.*

The mighty angel will announce to the world, in a voice that will shake the atmosphere, "Babylon is destroyed". The repeating of the fall of Babylon twice is to reveal the total destruction of the city. Further information is given, about this city, as being the place where the devil and demons have their dwelling place. The hold means a prison, or reserve, for fallen angels to await their being dispatched by Satan to carry out his wicked plans. A foul spirit speaks of some repulsive creature that is detestable in all its activities. Unclean and hateful is the character of a fallen angel, classified as a demon.

3. *For all nations have drunk of the wine of the wrath of her fornication, and the kings of the earth have committed fornication with her, and the merchants of the earth are waxed rich through the abundance of her delicacies.*

All nations of the earth participate in trade and commerce with Babylon. God's anger is motivated against Babylon because of fornication by the merchants who become interactive with the wicked system, which becomes their god, for profit making. The merchants are making gain by the products they take to the city, for sale, and profit, on cargo they take back to their country. The waxing rich is making an enormous amount of wealth in a short period of time. The power of desire for beautiful products, the world population is anxious to purchase, seems to create an intoxication for material wealth.

4. *And I heard another voice from heaven saying Come out of her, my people, that ye be not partakers of her sins, and that ye receive not of her plagues.*

Another command is heard from heaven to leave the city of Babylon, before the judgment of God falls upon them. God called for Lot, and his family, to leave the city of Sodom before He destroyed that wicked city. Genesis 19:15 "And when the morning arose, then the angels hastened Lot, saying, Arise, take thy wife, and thy two daughters, which are here; lest thou be consumed in the iniquity of the city." The first reason the angel gave, for God's people, to leave was to prevent them from becoming contaminated with the sins of Babylon. The second reason for leaving was to protect them from being slain when God destroyed the city with fire. A wonderful truth is evident when we see God caring for his children and seeking to protect them even though they may have been in the wrong place.

5. *For her sins have reached unto heaven, and God hath remembered her iniquities.*

The reason why God is going to destroy Babylon is because of the extent of their sins, which were so numerous and extremely depraved, that God took notice of such creatures who have fallen, so corrupt, in their ways. When people become so vial, in their sins, and also become defiant against God, and His Word, He cannot forget such iniquity and they are ready for destruction.

6. *Reward her even as she rewarded you, and double unto her double according to her works; in the cup which she hath filled fill to her double.*

Moses recorded in Exodus 22: 9 "For all manner of trespass, whether it be for ox, for ass, for sheep, for raiment, or for any manner of lost thing, which another challengeth to be his, the cause of both parties shall come before the judges; and whom the judges shall condemn, he shall pay double unto his neighbour." There are sins for which the criminal will restore double for their crimes. Babylon has sinned against Israel, by taking them into captivity, and many other crimes against them in war. Near the end of the tribulation period, God will destroy Babylon, and at this time, God will judge them and demand double restitution. In the cup of wrath, which Babylon poured out on other nations, God promises to mix a double cup of wrath to be poured out upon them in judgment, when the fire falls from heaven upon Babylon.

7. *How much she hath glorified herself, and lived deliciously, so much torment and sorrow give her: for she saith in her heart, I sit a queen, and am no widow, and shall see no sorrow.*

The depth of wickedness, of Babylon, is further seen by her being filled with pride; to live deliciously is be wanton or have a malicious attitude toward God. When judgment comes, Babylon will experience torment and sorrow, as they have caused others to suffer. Babylon sat as a queen and protected from the harsh lifestyle others have known and now torment and sorrow will be poured out in retribution. To see no sorrow is the capacity to commit dreadful crimes against others, and have no conviction or feel remorse for what you are doing.

8. *Therefore shall her plagues come in one day, death, and mourning, and famine; and she shall be utterly burned with fire: for strong is the Lord God who judgeth her.*

The judgment of God will be death, sorrow and famine upon the city that has inflicted, without remorse, these things upon others. Her plagues will fall upon the city at one time and without any warning about the doom awaiting them. To be utterly burned with fire is to be totally destroyed and every thing left in ruins. The power of Babylon is overtaken by the Omnipotent power of God who will judge her and exact punishment that is due for such atrocities she has committed. Isaiah 47:8 "Therefore hear now this, thou that art given to pleasures, that dwellest carelessly, that sayest in thine heart, I am, and none else beside me; I shall not sit as a widow, neither shall I know the loss of children: 9. But these two things shall come to thee in a moment in one day, the loss of children, and widowhood: they shall come upon thee in their perfection for the multitude of thy sorceries, and for the great abundance of thine enchantments."

9. *And the kings of the earth, who have committed fornication and lived deliciously with her, shall bewail her, and lament for her, when they shall see the smoke of her burning.*

The kings of the earth include most of the nations during the time of the tribulation period. The leaders of nations enter into a trade agreement with Babylon and, free trade, will be an inter relation of business known as fornication. To live deliciously is to partake of all the things the city of Babylon has to offer in trade, entertainment, and immorality. The merchants will be brought to tears because none of these, excitements of fleshly pleasure, will be there for them to enjoy. The smoke will drift upward as a reminder that sin is now being judged..

10. *Standing afar off for the fear of her torment, saying, Alas, alas that great city Babylon, that mighty city! for in one hour is thy judgment come.*

Merchants will be traveling overland, and by the river Euphrates, to reach the city of Babylon. The fire from heaven will erupt into such a conflagration that all traffic will stop and look upon a city of death and will be afraid to approach near because of the heat. Travelers will exclaim, alas, alas, some times understood as, woe, or pity be unto you. The volume of trade will classify Babylon to be called the mighty city. One hour is used to describe the very short time it takes for God to destroy the wicked city.

11. *And the merchants of the earth shall weep and mourn over her; for no man buyeth their merchandise any more.*

Again the Holy Spirit moved John to express the extent of the weeping and grief they have experienced, at the loss of Babylon. Many times, things are repeated to emphasize the deep emotional outcry, of grief, at the destruction they see. No more buying of merchandise is the reason why there is so much crying over the loss of profit which is no longer available.

12. *The merchandise of gold, and silver, and precious stones, and of pearls, and fine linen, and purple, and silk, and scarlet, and all thyine wood, and all manner vessels of ivory, and all manner vessels of most precious wood, and of brass, and iron, and marble,*

The quality of the goods sold, in Babylon, is noted by the costly material from which they were made. The list of the most precious materials is recorded in this verse. Gold and silver were rare materials and to have them made into the furniture would make it beautiful and costly. Precious stones would be enclosed in jewelry and, also, attached to garments of the very wealthy. Linen was the fabric, of the wealthy, to be used in the home or made into garments for men and women. Purple was one of the most beautiful colors, and much desired, for the dye used in their cloth. Silk was brought into the Mediterranean world by the Persians. Silk was a product of China, and at first, it was worn by the ladies, but in Roman times the men had garments made of silk. Scarlet is the color of crimson and the dye is extracted from the eggs of the insect, called kokkos, by the Greeks. Thyine wood is aromatic with a beautiful gain for making furniture. Ivory was sculptured into many articles for the home. Brass, iron, and marble were made into many useful containers for the kitchen and for storage of grain and other food.

13. *And cinnamon, and odours, and ointments, and frankincense, and wine, and oil, and fine flour, and wheat, and beasts, and sheep, and horses, and chariots, and slaves and souls of men.*

Cinnamon was used as a perfume, and placed in their beds, to fill the room with a delightful odor. Cinnamon was added to the holy oil for anointing in Old Testament days. Odors were made from a plant that grew in India and processed into an ointment. Frankincense is a plant grown in Persia and the extract, called galbanum, is a gum resin used as incense. The wine, oil, and fine flour, were in abundance, to satisfy the appetites of those who loved good food. All kind of animals were sold to meet the needs of farmers, and business men, of that day. Slaves for many purposes were available, to purchase, for the owners use. The souls of men could include those for illicit purposes.

14. *And the fruits that thy soul lusted after are departed from thee, and all things which were dainty and goodly are departed from thee, and thou shalt find them no more at all.*

    The Word of God uses ripe fruit from the tree to illustrate the most pleasurable things men will have taken from them, when Babylon is destroyed. All things dainty, in Greek, is oil rendered from animal fat, and applied to the skin, for an ointment, and used for polish on furniture to make it shine. Therefore, beautiful furniture for the home is something most desired. Goodly conveys the idea that things are elegant. All of the merchants are looking forward to desirable and beautiful products, to purchase, and return home and sell for much profit. All the precious commodities man may desire are now no longer available.

15. *The merchants of these things, which were made rich by them shall stand afar off for the fear of her torment, weeping and wailing,*

    It is possible that the merchants look upon the burning of Babylon and realize this is another judgment of God upon sinful men and be afraid to draw near the city knowing their lives could also be taken in the fire. As men look upon the city as it erupts into flames they know there is much torment or suffering to the inhabitants of Babylon. Weeping and wailing expresses the intense emotional feelings of the merchants who are frustrated and angry with God.

16. *And saying, Alas, alas, that great city, that was clothed in fine linen, and purple, and scarlet, and decked with gold, and precious stones and pearls!*

Alas has the meaning of woe, or grief, and the use of the word twice gives the connotation of much grief. John tells us about the beautiful and expensive clothing that will be worn in the city, with such wealth. The citizens and merchants of the city will be wearing the most decorated garments with golden threads interwoven into the fabric. Diamonds and precious jewels will be attached to the clothing, to make them sparkle with different colors.

17. *For in one hour so great riches is come to nought, And every shipmaster, and all the company in ships, and the sailors, and as many as trade by sea, stood afar off,*

God will rain fire upon the city of Babylon and the buildings will be engulfed in an inferno of flames of destruction, in one hour it is consumed into ashes. Nothing of any value can be salvaged from a city burning in a fire storm. The Euphrates River is navigable from the Persian Gulf to the city of Babylon. Many ships will be sailing, to and from the city, and many will be docked near the city. The ships that are some distance from the city will have their crew looking upon the raging fire of Babylon.

18. *And cried when they saw the smoke of her burning, saying, What city is like unto this great city!*

The merchants on their ships, with a loud voice, called out in grief that Babylon was a special city, which is unlike any other city of the world.

19. *And they cast dust on their heads, and cried, weeping and wailing, saying, Alas, alas, that great city, wherein were made rich all that had ships in the sea by reason of her costliness! for in one hour is she made desolate.*

When men would cast dust into their hair it was an expression of intense grief and anger. Often emotional grief was accompanied by shouts of anger from their soul. Weeping with tears of frustration would be associated with wailing, or grief, with intense feeling. Every one was concerned about the loss of their wealth, because of the destruction of Babylon, also, knowing the city may never be rebuilt, and become the trade center of the world.

20. *Rejoice over her, thou heaven, and ye holy apostles and prophets; for God hath avenged you on her.*

There was now rejoicing in Heaven because, this sin city, of extreme wickedness, is now destroyed by fire. Rejoicing is in response to a victory over Satan, and the destruction of his place of rule, from which many of the prophets and apostles have suffered and died. God is now bringing judgment upon a city, for its past sins, against those who love and follow the Lord.

21. *And a mighty angel took up a stone like a great millstone, and cast it into the sea, saying, Thus with violence shall that great city Babylon be thrown down, and shall be found no more at all.*

The Holy Spirit breathed upon John to use an illustration to describe the destruction of Babylon. A millstone is round and weighs several hundred pounds. If an angel threw a millstone into the sea, it would make a great splash, and in an instant it would disappear. The city of Babylon fell, like a great splash, and vanished, never again to be rebuilt.

22. *And the voice of harpers, and musicians, and of pipers, and trumpeters, shall be heard no more at all in thee; and no craftsman, of whatsoever craft he be, shall be found any more in thee; and the sound of a millstone shall be heard no more at all in thee;*

First mentioned is the end of the entertainment, which is always so much a part, of the opulent society of Babylon. The harpers are those who played the lyre, the pipers were men and women who played the flute. A trumpet was an instrument made from a goat or ram's horn. The music of instruments, and the vocalist, was no longer heard in the city. The second mentioned to be destroyed was the skilled artisan who was skilled in making some of the most beautiful products ever made. There will be a wide range of manufactured furniture people, around the world, will desire to purchase, at any price. The third area of destruction is that of manufacturing facilities represented by the sound of the millstone that ceases to be heard. A city of joy and delight, to the lost who have taken the mark of the beast, will never again be experienced by the ungodly.

23. *And the light of a candle shall shine no more at all in thee; and the voice of the bridegroom and of the bride shall be heard no more at all in thee: for they merchants were the great men of the earth; for by thy sorceries were all nations deceived.*

The light of the candle tells us that this city was open all night for entertainment, and all types, of sinful pleasures. The city of Babylon will carry on business day and night, to enhance the profit making. The excitement of marriage, and the laughter, that accompanies a wedding will never again be a part of the activities of Babylon. Jeremiah 25:10 "Moreover I will take from them the voice of mirth, and the voice of gladness, the voice of the bridegroom, and the voice of; the bride, the sound of the millstones, and the light of the candle."

The merchants, who were called great men, are known as princes in the original language of the New Testament, although, today they would be known as wealthy business men. The magician was using deceptive deals to enhance their wealth which extended to deceiving the nations around the world.

24. *And in her was found the blood of prophets, and of saints, and of all that were slain upon the earth.*

History has recorded the wars of Babylon that have been waged against Israel. Many deaths have occurred, by these wars, and more died when Israel was taken captive by Babylon. All through out history, many of God's people have died because of the determined effort of Babylon, the place where Satan dwells, to destroy those who serve the true God. Jeremiah 51:49 "As Babylon hath caused the slain of Israel to fall, so at Babylon shall fall the slain of all the earth"

Chapter XIX

Introduction: The focus of this chapter is the destruction of all armies, and the nations, who invade Israel, in the final phase of the Battle of Armageddon. Verses one through four, the Holy Spirit breathes upon John to praise the Lord, our God, because, He moves to judge sin and the evil Satan has encouraged his followers to commit. Verses five and six, praise God who is ruling and reigning over all the earth. Verses seven through nine, the marriage of the Lamb of God, and the marriage supper, are seen as a time of great blessing for all of mankind. Verses eleven through nineteen, Jesus comes to the earth and wages war against the armies of the goat nations. Jesus, the Son of God, tramples the armies and speaks the command which destroys all the nations who have sent their soldiers to war against God's people Israel. The chapter ends with the casting of the antichrist, and the anti- Holy Spirit, into the lake of fire called hell.

1. *And after these things I heard a great voice of much people in heaven, saying, Alleluia; Salvation, and glory, and honour, and power, unto the Lord our God:*

    After the judgments of the Seven Sealed Book have been carried out, and the redemption of the earth has been completed, all of God's people, in heaven, join in anthems of praise to the Lord our God. At this time, the souls of the Old Testament saints are now in heaven. The New Testament Church, the Bride of Christ, is in heaven with their glorified resurrected bodies. Also, included in heaven are the tribulation saints who have been martyred for their faith, in Jesus the Son of God. All together, the redeemed of the earth praise and worship the Lord our God, because He is worthy. Jesus has saved every one who is in Heaven and has loved each one with a divine love called grace, and has securely kept all believers safe, and secure, by His power.

2. *For true and righteous are his judgments: for he hath judged the great whore, which did corrupt the earth with her fornication, and hath avenged the blood of his servants at her hand.*

Jesus is truth, in contrast to all that is evil; an example is, Jesus is the true God and all other gods are false. Jesus is just in all of His dealings with man, and will extend mercy, when the sinner repents and asks Him for mercy, to save them. Jesus will justly judge the apostate counterfeit religious system, of Satan, and move Satan to destroy his own power structure, of deception. The great whore forced the rulers of Europe during the dark ages, to submit to the power of Romanism, in order to hold their throne. Another reason the Lord will destroy the false religion is because during the time, of the Dark Ages, in Europe many were martyred for their faith in Jesus alone to save them. Some records of history, have recorded, the most brutal deaths occurred to believers by the inquisition, promoted by the apostate church. God moves with justice, to deal with this whore, because, of the terrible crimes they committed against God's people.

3. *And again they said, Alleluia. And her smoke rose up for ever and ever.*

They represents the much people recorded in verse one. The great throng of the redeemed in heaven join in an anthem of praise of worship to God. All of heaven is rejoicing, because, God has destroyed Babylon, that wicked city. Smoke arising for ever and ever gives the connotation that the destruction of Babylon is final and will never exist again forever.

Isaiah 34:10 It shall not be quenched night nor day; the smoke thereof shall go up for ever: from generation to generation it shall lie waste; none shall pass through it for ever and ever.

4. *And the four and twenty elders and the four beasts fell down and worshipped God that sat on the throne, saying, Amen; Alleluia.*

The twenty four elders were men who were redeemed, and now are in heaven, representing, the Old Testament Tribes, and the New Testament Apostles. The four living creatures were created by God and they will carry out all commands God directs to order man and animals to do His will. All of the saints in heaven join together in obeisance, and praise, to Jehovah because He has destroyed the wicked city of Babylon, who corrupted the whole earth with her sins.

5. *And a voice came out of the throne, saying, Praise our God, all ye his servants, and ye that fear him, both small and great.*

Verses five and six, the inhabitants, or servants, in heaven are praising God, because, He is on the throne, and in control, of all things in heaven and on earth. Those who fear the Lord are those who recognize Him as a Holy and Righteous God, of perfect Deity. The fear of God is reverential awe in light of who we are, as human beings in the presence of an Omnipotent God. Small and great includes all of mankind regardless of their rank or social status.

6. *And I heard as it were the voice of a great multitude, and as the voice of many waters, and as the voice of mighty thunderings, saying, Alleluia: for the Lord God Omnipotent reigneth.*

John is using terms that describe a power so great that men tremble with fear at their sound. The voice of an army shouting outside the city walls was a fearful sound. The raging sound of a rushing torrent of water, down a valley toward a village was frightening, because it brought death. Thundering that shook the atmosphere was evidence of expending great power, beyond man's control. All types of power, man has experienced, cannot compare with the power of God. All things in heaven, and on the earth, are under the complete power of God, who can do all things according to His will.

7. *Let us be glad and rejoice, and give honour to him: for the marriage of the Lamb is come, and his wife hath made herself ready.*

All of the saints and angels in heaven will rejoice when the New Testament Church, the Bride of Christ, is married to Jesus. The marriage relationship will unite the New Testament Believers to become one with Jesus, as a marriage makes the husband and wife to become one in God's sight.

Some day soon, the Lord Jesus is coming near to the earth and calls His bride to meet Him in the air. Jesus will take his bride to Heaven and the marriage of the Lamb will take place in the presence of God. II Corinthians 11:2 "For I am jealous over you with godly jealous: for I have espoused you to one husband, that I may present you as a chaste virgin to Christ." The bride of Christ hath made herself ready by accepting Jesus to be their Lord and Saviour and, at the time of the new birth, the Lord does a work of grace in us known as justification. Ephesians 5:27 "That he might present it to himself a glorious church, not having spot, or wrinkle, or any such thing; but that it should be holy and without blemish."

8. *And to her was granted that she should be arrayed in fine linen, clean and white: for the fine linen is the righteousness of saints.*

In the days of the New Testament linen was the finest quality of material for clothing. Kings and wealthy people wore clothes of linen and the Holy Spirit uses this analogy to inform us that the garments for the Bride of Christ will be the most beautiful garment found in heaven. Clean and white depict the purity of the Bride of Christ who have all their sins forgiven and are now clothed about with the righteousness of the Lord Jesus Christ. The righteousness of the saints could not be something we have earned, but it is that which was imputed to us at the moment we are saved.

9. *And he saith unto me, Write, Blessed are they which are called unto the marriage supper of the Lamb. And he saith unto me, These are the true sayings of God.*

A Hebrew wedding, during the time when our Lord was on the earth was conducted in the bridegroom's home. The wedding, in the home, was attended by the immediate family and was usually performed some time in the afternoon. Some time after the wedding, the bride and groom would walk a predetermined route to the banquet hall. Those who were invited to the marriage supper, would wait along the street, and join the procession to the marriage supper. Those who were dress in the wedding garment, and had oil in their lamp for lighting, were permitted enter the wedding feast. If the parents were wealthy, the wedding supper might last for several days. Matthew 25: 6 "And at midnight there was a cry made, Behold, the bridegroom cometh; go ye out to meet him. 10. And while they went to buy, the bridegroom came; and they that were ready went in with him to the marriage (feast) and the door was shut"

They who were called to the marriage supper were the Old Testament Saints. John the Baptist died before the resurrection of Jesus from the grave and, therefore, he died under the period of the Law. Those who trusted Jesus, and died, after the resurrection of Jesus made up the bride of Christ. John the Apostle wrote about John the Baptist in John 3:29 "He that hath the bride is the bridegroom: but the friend of the bridegroom, which standeth and heareth him, rejoiceth greatly because of the bridegroom's voice: this my joy therefore if fulfilled." John the Baptist died before Jesus was crucified and was not included in the New Testament Church, as part of the bride of Christ. John the Baptist rejoiced because he saw and heard the bridegroom.

Some day soon, Jesus will take His bride to heaven where the marriage will take place. The tribulation period will start on the earth, and at the end of the tribulation, Jesus and His bride will come back to this earth to set up the millennial rule and reign on earth. The souls of the Old Testament saints were taken to heaven when Jesus rose from the grave. At the setting up of the millennium, the Old Testament Saints will be resurrected, and given a glorified body. Daniel 12: 1 "And at that time shall Michael stand up, the great prince which standeth for the children of thy people: and there shall be a time of trouble, such as never was since there was a nation even to that same time: and at that time thy people shall be delivered, every one that shall be found written in the book. 2. And many of them that sleep in the dust of the earth shall awake, some to everlasting life, and some to shame and everlasting contempt."

10. *And I fell at his feet to worship him. And he said unto me, See thou do it not: I am thy fellow-servant, and of thy brethren that have the testimony of Jesus: worship God: for the testimony of Jesus is the spirit of prophecy.*

John was so excited and filled with rejoicing, by what he had heard and seen, that he fell down before the angel who had been instructing him about things in heaven. The angel responded that he was not Deity and was not to be worshiped. The angel gave the reason why he was not to be worshiped is because he was a created creature of God. The angel informed John I am a servant, as you are a servant of God, and I am no different than your brethren who were also created by God. Jesus taught His disciples, and it is recorded in the Bible that Believers are now to proclaim the prophecy about the Lord Jesus Christ.

11. *And I saw heaven opened, and behold a white horse; and he that sat upon him was called Faithful and True, and in righteousness he doth judge and make war.*

John was again permitted to see into heaven and he saw a white horse and upon the horse was the Son of God, in the splendor of His glory. Jesus is faithful to keep all of His promises and, always, speaks the truth. Jesus has never done any thing wrong and never will do any thing that is unjust. When man evaluates all the devastating, destructive, judgments of the tribulation period, man may question the motives of God, when He destroys nations who rise up against his people, Israel. God will judge the world, because of sin, and at the same time do what is just and right in all that He does. Every one who takes the mark of the beast and is lost will be judged on the basis of justice.. The Lord Jesus would have given every person mercy, and saved every one of the lost, during the tribulation period, but those who refuse mercy, and choose to follow Satan, will endure the justice of God. The justice for the ungodly may be severe, but, it is what they deserve, because of their wicked sins against God and His followers.

12. *His eyes were as a flame of fire, and on his head were many crowns; and he had a name written, that no man knew, but he himself.*

When an object is heated, with fire, heat penetrates the entire material. The eyes of Jesus, like fire, will penetrate through the veneer, and see what is in the depths of our heart or soul. The many crowns, worn by Jesus, tell us that Jesus is, King of kings, and Lord of lords, over all of the heavens and earth. During the Millennium Jesus will rule as king, over the whole world, from the throne of David established in Jerusalem. Jesus will take a name that He only will know to designate His authority and power over all the world.

13. *And he was clothed with a vesture dipped in blood: and his name is called The Word of God.*

In verse fifteen we have an indication about where the blood, on His vesture, came from. During the last phase of the Battle of Armageddon the armies from the north, south, and east will marshal their forces against Israel, and be led to believe they can destroy Israel, before God can intervene. When the armies, from the goat nations, fight their way into Jerusalem, the Lord Jesus will come from heaven and trample these soldiers as if you trampled grapes in the winevat. This is the blood that will stain His vesture when He crushes the bodies of the soldiers. Isaiah 63:2 "Wherefore art thou red in thine apparel, and thy garments like him that treadeth in the winevat? 3. I have trodden the winepress alone; and of the people there was none with me: for I will tread them in mine anger, and trample them in my fury; and their blood shall be sprinkled upon my garments, and I will stain all my raiment."

In the gospel of John, chapter one and verse one, Jesus is called the Word of God. All that Jesus said is the truth and all that is recorded in the Bible is truth which stands forever unchanged. Jesus is the Word of God.

14. *And the armies which were in heaven followed him upon white horses, clothed in fine linen, white and clean.*

The army is in heaven, clothed in fine linen, white and clean, identifies them in verse eight, as the bride of Christ. It is the bride of Christ, who has been resurrected, with a glorified body, and ready to return back to this earth and set up the millennial kingdom. The bride of Christ has been promised, to forever be with Him, after we have been caught away, to meet the Lord in the air. This army must be the bride of Christ accompanied with angels. I Thessalonians 4:17 "Then we which are alive and remain shall be caught up together with them in the clouds, to meet the Lord in the air: and so shall we ever be with the Lord."

15. *And out of his mouth goeth a sharp sword, that with it he should smite the nations: and he shall rule them with a rod* *of iron: and he treadeth the winepress of the fierceness and wrath of Almighty God.*

The sharp sword is the Word of God being spoken in judgment upon the goat nations. Revelations 1:16 "And he had in his right hand seven stars: and out of his mouth went a sharp two-edged sword: and his countenance was as the sun shineth in his strength." Isaiah 11:4 "But with righteousness shall he judge the poor, and reprove with equity for the meek of the earth: and he shall smite the earth with the rod of his mouth, and with the breath of his lips shall he slay the wicked."

The nations that will be destroyed, at the end of the tribulation period, will be the goat nations. The goat nations are those that have given the control of their armies to the antichrist, and have invaded Israel, to destroy them and their nation. After Jesus tramples the army of the antichrist, He will then speak the word, and all citizens of each goat nation will die. A rod is used by a potter, to crush any defective vessel, and cast the pieces aside. The defeat of the ungodly nations will be a crushing, like a potter would do to destroy something worthless.

The treading down of the wicked army will be so crushing, that blood will flow from the bodies of men, like a running stream of water down the valley. Revelation 14:20 "And the winepress was trodden without the city, and blood came out of the wine press, even unto the horse bridles, by the space of a thousand and six hundred furlongs." (two hundred miles)

16. *And he hath on his vesture and on his thigh a name written, KING OF KINGS, AND LORD OF LORDS.*

Upon the garments worn by the Lord Jesus will have a title, inscribed the King and only true King, and the only Lord of Deity, and none other liken unto Him. Jesus will be the only King who will rule from the throne of David during the Millennium. Daniel 2:47 "The king answered unto Daniel, and said, Of a truth it is, that your God is a God of gods, and a Lord of kings, and a revealer of secrets, seeing thou couldest reveal this secret."

17. *And I saw an angel standing in the sun; and he cried with a loud voice, saying to all the fowls that fly in the midst of heaven, Come and gather yourselves together unto the supper of the great God;*

An angel standing in the sun suggests the shining of the glory of God was about him, in such brilliance, that he appeared to be in the light of the sun. One angel proclaims to the flesh-eating birds to gather, on the battle field, and feast themselves upon the flesh of the fallen soldiers, who have been trampled by the Lord Jesus. The supper of the great God conveys the idea of, a feast so great that it will take days for the vultures to consume all the flesh they desire.

18. *That ye may eat the flesh of kings, and the flesh of captains, and the flesh of mighty men, and the flesh of horses, and of them that sit on them, and the flesh of all men, both free and bond, both small and great.*

Men from the rulers of nations to the poorest of the peasants will be enlisted in the army of the antichrist and be killed in the conflict. No one will survive and live because of their social rank or place of power in their nation. God is not a respecter of persons and those who choose to fight against God in the Battle of Armageddon will be slain when Jesus issues an order for them to perish in death, for their following the antichrist, in their effort to destroy Israel..

19. *And I saw the beast, and the kings of the earth, and their armies, gather together to make war against him that sat on the horse, and against his army.*

John will identify those who lead their armies against God, and his people Israel, to be the followers of the beast known as the antichrist. The war is between God and the devil, who enlists the nations, of the world, to help him overthrow God. The beast is enlisted, by the Devil, to wage war and defeat the forces of heaven. Jesus engages Himself into the conflict and He alone destroys all military personnel of all nations involved.

He that sat on the horse is the Lord Jesus, recorded in verse eleven as the one riding upon a white horse.

20. *And the beast was taken, and with him the false prophet that wrought miracles before him, with which he deceived them that had received the mark of the beast, and them that worshipped his image. These both were cast alive into a lake of fire burning with brimstone.*

At the very end of the tribulation period, the antichrist was taken, with a firm grasp, most likely, by an angel, and cast into hell Also, another member of the unholy trinity, the anti holy spirit, was cast into the lake of fire. This false prophet performed many miracles, which seemed to convey the idea, that he was supernatural, and could do things equal to God. The performance of these miracles was permitted by God, to further deceive those who had taken the mark of the beast. These both together, were cast into the lake of fire called hell. God has now banished two members of the unholy trinity, and will later cast Satan into the lake of fire, at the end of the millennial period.

21. *And the remnant were slain with the sword of him that sat upon the horse, which sword proceeded out of his mouth: and all the fowls were filled with their flesh.*

All human creatures who, are from the goat nations, will perish with their armies. Jesus trampled the soldiers, and now, Jesus speaks, a command, and every person living in those goat nations will die. The birds of prey will, also, feast upon the bodies since there was no one left to bury the dead.

Chapter XX

Introduction: In the previous chapter, two members of the unholy trinity were cast alive into the lake of fire. Chapter twenty informs us that Satan himself will be apprehended, and cast into the bottomless pit. Satan will be released from the bottomless pit, at the end of the millennium, for a short period of time. When Satan is released from the bottomless pit he will deceive some of the young people, who have been born during the millennial period. Satan will then lead those he has deceived to overpower the Lord Jesus, and His government, and take the New Jerusalem. God will rain fire upon Satan's army and destroy it. After the rebellion, Satan will be cast into the lake of fire known as the eternal hell. At the end of the millennium, all of the lost will receive a resurrected body, and be called to stand before the Great White Throne where the Lord Jesus will be their judge and they will then be sentenced to the lake of fire.

1. *And I saw an angel come down from heaven, having the key of the bottomless pit and a great chain in his hand.*

    An arch angel was dispatched, from heaven, to apprehend Satan and put him in the bottomless pit, located in the center of the earth. This mighty angel was given a key, or authority, to open the pit and, a chain for the purpose of binding Satan, and rendering him helpless, to resist, being arrested.

2. *And he laid hold on the dragon, that old serpent, which is the Devil, and Satan, and bound him a thousand years,*

To lay hold upon Satan is, to arrest him, and put him away for one thousand years, while the Lord Jesus rules this earth for a millennium. Some names are given to Satan which will reflect his character. Satan is called a dragon, which means to look or to see, as a creature of beauty. Ezekiel 28:12 "Son of man, take up a lamentation upon the king of Tyrus, and say unto him, Thus saith the Lord God; Thou sealest up the sum, full of wisdom, and perfect in beauty." The old serpent is one who is crooked and existed before man was created. The name devil tells us that Satan is one who slanders man to God and God to man. Satan is the accuser of the saints of God and the adversary of all of humanity.

3. *And cast him into the bottomless pit, and shut him up, and set a seal upon him, that he should deceive the nations no more, till the thousand years should be fulfilled: and after that he must be loosed a little season.*

The mighty angel of God cast Satan into the bottomless pit. If the pit is deep enough, to be near the center of the earth, gravitation would be the same in all directions, and a weightless condition would exist and no bottom could be experienced. To shut Satan up is to make it impossible for Satan to escape his prison. Sitting a seal is the security that no one could open the pit, without God's permission. The reason why Satan is banished into the pit is to make it impossible for him, to accost any person, and lead them to commit any sinful acts. Satan will be contained, in the bottomless pit, for one thousand years, and then God will permit him to be released, for a short period of time and roam the earth once again.

4. *And I saw thrones, and they sat upon them, and judgment was given unto them: and I saw the souls of them that were beheaded for the witness of Jesus, and for the word of God, and which had not worshipped the beast, neither his image, neither had received his mark upon their foreheads, or in*

their hands; and they lived and reigned with Christ a thousand years.

John writes about thrones which would indicate, perhaps, as many as twenty four thrones, found recorded in chapter four. They that sat upon the thrones are those who have already been given power, and authority, to rule with Christ. Judgment was already given to them, who sat on the thrones, in carrying out the judgments recorded in the, Seven Sealed Book of Redemption, for the world. In light, of the fact, that those on the thrones have already assumed power to rule must be the twenty four elders. Revelation 4:4 "And round about the throne were four and twenty seats: and upon the seats I saw four and twenty elders sitting, clothed in white raiment; and they had on their heads crowns of gold."

John sees another of the terrible crimes, committed by the antichrist in his effort, during the tribulation period, to destroy the witness of Christ. The tribulation saints had their heads chopped off by something resembling an ax. The martyrs were those who were saved, through the ministry, of the one hundred and forty and four thousand evangelists our Lord sealed to be His witnesses. If any one trusted Jesus to be their Saviour, they would be killed if they gave a testimony of being saved, or that they believed the Word of God to be true, and had refused to take the mark of the beast

One of the wonderful blessings, for those who suffer such indignities, is to know they will live and reign with Christ during the millennium. The tribulation martyrs will never again suffer, at the hands of Satan, the brutal treatment they experienced during the Tribulation Period..

5. *But the rest of the dead lived not again until the thousand years were finished. This is the first resurrection.*

The dead are those, who are lost, without embracing the atonement God required, either in the Old Testament or New Testament Period. During the time of the Law, it was demanded that the people bring a lamb without spot or blemish, to be offered by faith, looking forward until the time the promised Messiah would come, to the earth. Jesus did come as the promised messiah and made the proper atonement, for the whole world, and man now accepts by faith, this atonement Jesus made on the cross.

The dead who are lost will not be resurrected for another thousand years after the tribulation is over. When the lost die their souls go to Hades and are held there until the end of the millennium. The lost are resurrected and given a body that fire will not destroy and this is the first resurrection, for the lost people of all ages.

6. *Blessed and holy is he that hath part in the first resurrection: on such the second death hath no power, but they shall be priests of God and of Christ, and shall reign with him a thousand years.*

Jesus was the first resurrection from the dead. All of mankind is made to rejoice, and to be considered fortunate, when they are declared to be Holy, by receiving Jesus as their Lord and Saviour. To have part in the first resurrection is to accept Jesus who was crucified, buried and was the first one who was resurrected with a glorified body. The born again believer will some day die physically, if the rapture, for believers, does not happen in their life time. The second death is often said to be the banishment, of the lost soul, from Jesus and heaven, never to know the blessings of salvation. A child of God, who has been born again, will never be lost and cast into darkness, and hell, and endure the second death

Every saved person will have a place of service, in the millennium, and have some office of government, to rule with Christ, during this time of thousand years.

7. *And when the thousand years are expired, Satan shall be loosed out of his prison,*

At the end of the millennium, Satan will be released out of the bottomless pit, and come to the surface of the earth. Satan does not escape out of the bottomless pit, God permits him to be released so he may carry out his last attempt to overthrow God, in a power struggle, where Satan fails, and then he is cast into hell.

8. *And shall go out to deceive the nations which are in the four quarters of the earth, Gog and Magog, to gather them together to battle: the number of whom is as the sand of the sea.*

The nations, Satan is able to deceive, are human beings who have been born during the millennium. At the end of the tribulation period, those people who have not taken the mark of the beast and have trusted Jesus, to save them, at His revelation, will be permitted to enter the millennium alive. Matthew 10:22 "And ye shall be hated of all men for my name's sake: but he that endureth to the end shall be saved." The scripture is telling us about the conditions of the tribulation period and a promise to live through out the millennium is given to those who trust Jesus, to save them, and refuse to believe the devil. Those individuals who have been saved, and manage to survive, until the end of the tribulation period, will be saved to go into the millennium as human beings. The conditions of the earth, in the millennium, will be much like it was during the time of the Garden of Eden. There will be no sickness, no pain in child bearing, and no child born during the millennium will die if within one hundred years if they trust Jesus to save them. Isaiah 33:24 "And the inhabitant shall not say, I am sick: the people that dwell therein shall be forgiven their iniquity." Every one who is saved, and enters the millennium, will not die, and the children born to these human beings will also live through the millennium, if they trust Jesus by faith to save them. Each child born to human beings will die at one hundred years old, and be lost, if they do not trust Jesus to save them by faith. Isaiah 65:20 "There shall be no more thence an infant of days, nor an old man that hath not filled his days: for the child shall die an hundred years old; but the sinner being an hundred years old shall be accursed."

Society continues to say, that a child's environment is the cause of their sins, and because of that, they are not responsible for their sinful behavior. In the millennium, children will be born in a perfect environment where there will be no one practicing sin. Satan will not be here to entice them to sin; they will have only their sinful fallen nature, and some of them will refuse to trust Jesus to save them. The real problem for man is not his environment but it is their wicked fallen nature, that causes them to become criminals and to be lost. Jesus will give human beings an opportunity to see the real source of man's problem is his fallen nature.

In a perfect environment, where there is no sickness, and no pain in child bearing, will see an explosion of the population, who will be alive at the end of the millennium. Millions of children, who are less than one hundred years old, and have not trusted Jesus as their Saviour, will be the ones who Satan will tempt to follow him. The young people who have never been subject to the temptations of the devil, and the lost world, will be vulnerable to the lies of Satan and believe him.

9. *And they went up on the breadth of the earth and compassed the camp of the saints about, and the beloved city: and fire came down from God out of heaven, and devoured them.*

Those who went up on the vast expanse of the earth were the millions of young people, born in the millennium, who had not yet accepted Jesus as their Saviour. The propaganda, of Satan, is so convincing they will followed him. These young people were dealing with the fallen adamic nature they were born with, and living under the rule, of the saints of God, was restricting their life so they were not permitted to practice the sins their sinful nature desire. The children, who were living to satisfy the flesh, were eager to escape Christian rule and follow Satan and his promise to permit them to live after the lust of the flesh.

Satan's plan of attack was to circle the New Jerusalem, the city where the bride of Christ lived. Satan led this massive throng of people to storm the beautiful city Jesus had prepared for His bride. When Satan and his army approached the city that came down from heaven, God rained fire upon them, and burned every one of them to ashes. The defeat of Satan will take place at the end of the millennium. The bride of Christ is on the earth, ruling and reigning with Christ, and we then will walk upon the ashes, of millions of people, Satan led astray and now are destroyed. Malachi 4:1 "For, behold, the day cometh, that shall burn as an oven; and all the proud, yea, and all that do wickedly, shall be stubble: and the day that cometh shall burn them up, saith the Lord of hosts, that it shall leave them neither root nor branch. 3. And ye shall tread down the wicked; for they shall be ashes under the soles of your feet in the day that I shall do this, saith the Lord of hosts."

10. *And the devil that deceived them was cast into the lake of fire and brimstone, where the beast and the false prophet are, and shall be tormented day and night for ever and ever.*

The devil was created, as an archangel, and had a wonderful place in heaven. After Satan sinned he was cast out of heaven and was permitted to dwell on the earth. When Adam and Eve were created, by God, Satan deceived them to sin, and because of this, God placed a curse upon him. God proclaimed to Adam and Eve that the Messiah would cause his defeat. Genesis 3:15 "And I will put enmity between thee and the woman, and between thy seed and her seed; it shall bruise thy head, and thou shalt bruise his heel." At the end of the millennium, time has come for Satan to be cast into hell, where he will remain forever. The lake of fire, superheated with brimstone, called hell, is the place God created to punish Satan. The beast or antichrist and false prophet known as the anti holy spirit were the first ones, at the end of the tribulation, to be cast into the lake of fire. The time of their torment in hell is forever, and there will never be a moment of time Satan will escape the heat and suffering of hell.

11. *And I saw a great white throne, and him that sat on it, from whose face the earth and the heaven fled away; and there was found no place for them.*

The great white throne judgment will take place after the millennium. The great white throne suggest that it is one of splendor, and majesty, befitting the sovereign who will occupy the throne. A white throne is the symbol of purity, and a place of justice. Jesus is the judge who will be seated on the throne, judging the lost people, of all ages. John 5:22 "For the Father judgeth no man, but committed all judgment unto the Son:" There seems to be nothing found in the Word of God that would suggest that believers will view this judgment scene or be called to testify.

The lost people will be resurrected, and given a body that will forever exist, and cannot be destroyed, in the lake of fire. The Lord Jesus will call the lost to approach the white throne, and it appears, that the earth is fleeing away, would place the throne some where in space. Standing before Jesus, to be judged in space, would leave no place for any one to hide. The lost person will now stand alone, to face their sins, and see the glorified, Holy and righteous, Son of God. All lost souls will see the glory of the Saviour, they rejected, and will conclude they deserve nothing less, than to be cast into hell.

12. *And I saw the dead, small and great, stand before God; and the books were opened: and another book was opened, which is the book of life: and the dead were judged out of those things which were written in the books, according to their works.*

Small and great, includes all sinners, of all social rank, from the poorest to the richest. No one will be excluded from the great white throne judgment. There are two sets of books in heaven; one set is called the book of life, and every person born has their name recorded in this book; the other set of books is called, the book of life eternal, or the Lamb's book of life. When a person reaches the age they are accountable to

God, for how they live, their sins are recorded in the book of life. The blood atonement of Jesus Christ is the only way this sin record can be blotted out. The lost person, who has never trusted Jesus to save them, will have all their sins before them, written in the book of life to condemn them. Jesus will open the book of life eternal, before the lost person, to assure them they never accepted Jesus as their Lord and Saviour. The lost person with their sins, still recorded, will be condemned already by their record. The spiritually dead, lost, person will be judged by the things recorded against them in the book of life. There seems to be two types of punishment in hell. First, the physical suffering will be the same for every lost person in hell. There will not be hotter or cooler places in hell, the heat will be the same for all in the lake of fire. Second there is mental anguish, to relive forever, the experience of the suffering and horror experienced by all the victims of their crimes. Those lost people, who have committed no vicious crimes, will not suffer the mental anguish of weeping and wailing, and gnashing of teeth, like those who are now insane by thinking about the dreadful crimes they have committed. Lost people will remember, in hell, about things that happened on earth. Luke 16:25 "But Abraham said, Son, remember that thou in thy lifetime receivedst thy good things, and likewise Lazarus evil things: but now he is comforted, and thou art tormented."

13. *And the sea gave up the dead which were in it; and death and hell delivered up the dead which were in them: and they were judged every man according to their works.*

Those who were buried in the sea, and consumed by sea creatures, will be resurrected when Jesus calls for them to be judged. This verse teaches us, that all will be resurrected regardless of the place a person was buried. Every person will be called from the grave to receive a new body, whether saved, or lost. The souls of the lost, who are in Hades, will be united with a resurrected body, to stand before the Lord Jesus Christ, and be judged at the Great White Throne Judgment.

Again the Word of God makes a clear statement that the lost will suffer mental anguish, in relation to the crimes they have committed. When a lost person comes to the white throne, they will have all their sins before them, written in the books which are the same as a written confession of their guilt. At the time of judging the lost, Jesus as God, will not have to condemn one soul to hell; every lost person is already condemned by their own record as recorded in the book of life. In the Gospel of John 3:18 we see the sinner already condemned when they come to be judged. "He that believeth on him is not condemned: but he that believeth not is condemned already, because he hath not believed in the name of the only begotten Son of God."

14. *And death and hell were cast into the lake of fire, This is the second death.*

All who die without being forgiven of their sins, will after they are judged, be cast or thrown into the lake of fire called hell. To be cast or thrown into hell, indicates they will be going through space, to reach the place of the lake of fire. A lost person is one who refuses to trust Jesus to save them, and to go to heaven. There will be only two places to go after the judgment, that is, either, heaven or hell. If a lost person refuses to go to heaven, by the way of the atonement, there is no other place for the lost to go, but to the lake of fire. The second death is to be eternally separated from God, with no hope for salvation. It is a state of existence, where the person lives in a condition, of continually dying but be never experiences death and dying.

15. *And whosoever was not found written in the book of life was cast into the lake of fire.*

Any person, who does not have their name recorded in the Lamb's book of Life, at the moment of salvation, will be lost and will be rejected and cast into the lake of fire. In order to be qualified to go to heaven, a person first must be born physically, which places your name in the book of life. When a person is born again spiritually, their name is recorded in the Lamb's book of life, which assures that saved soul will be admitted to heaven. If a soul stands before Jesus, with their name only found in the book of life, with a record of all their sins, that person is lost and condemned already to the lake of fire.

Chapter XXI

Introduction: At the end of the millennium, John writes a wonderful truth about the creation, of a new heaven, and a new earth. In verse two, John describes the New Jerusalem Jesus went to heaven to prepare for His bride. John 14:2. "In my Father's house are many mansions; if it were not so, I would have told you. 3. And if I go and prepare a place for you, I will come again, and receive you unto myself; that where I am, there ye may be also."

Verses three, through seven, inform the believer, about many blessings, of being with the Lord Jesus in heaven. There is a warning, in verse eight, to those who are evil of heart, and commit wicked sins, that they will be cast into hell. The invitation, in verse nine, is given by an angel for John to come with him and see the bride of Christ. Starting in verse ten, John sees the Holy City, the New Jerusalem that will come back with Jesus, and His bride, when He returns to the earth, at the end of the tribulation period. The rest of the chapter describes this beautiful city Jesus is now preparing, in heaven, for His bride.

1. *And I saw a new heaven and a new earth: for the first heaven and the first earth were passed away; and there was no more sea.*

After the millennium, God will speak, and the earth that is now under a curse, will be destroyed. II Peter 3:12 "Looking for and hasting unto the coming of the day of God, wherein the heavens being on fire shall be dissolved, and the elements shall melt with fervent heat?" After Adam and Eve sinned,

Satan, man, and the earth, were cursed and experienced the consequences of this curse. Genesis 3:17 "And unto Adam he said, Because thou hast hearkened unto the voice of thy wife, and hast eaten of the tree, of which I commanded thee, saying, Thou shalt not eat of it: cursed is the ground for thy sake; in sorrow shalt thou eat of it all the days of thy life;". This earth is not a suitable place of the New Jerusalem to settle upon, or a place for the bride of Christ to dwell. Isaiah was informed about the creation of, a new heaven, and a new earth. Isaiah 66:22 "For as the new heavens and the new earth, which I will make, shall remain before me, saith the Lord, so shall your seed and your name remain." Isaiah records that God will create, in the future, a new heaven and earth; also, the new one will never be destroyed. The word new, in Greek, means something recently made and has never been used or defiled. In Matthew 27:60 The same word new is used when describing the new tomb of Joseph, which had been recently constructed, and had never been used. In the creating of a new heaven and earth God will not become involved with any exercise of energy. God must only speak and things will come into existence. Psalm 33:6 "By the word of the Lord were the heavens made; and all the host of them by the breath of his mouth." There will not be a sea on the new earth, which some believe to mean there will never be any unrest of troubled souls in heaven.

2. *And I John saw the holy city, new Jerusalem, coming down from God out of heaven, prepared as a bride adorned for her husband.*

John now turns his attention to describing a beautiful city Jesus is now preparing for His bride. John 14:2 "In my Father's house are many mansions: if it were not so, I would have told you. I go to prepare a place for you. 3. And if I go and prepare a place for you, I will come again, and receive you unto myself; that where I am, there ye may be also."

At the end of the tribulation period, the New Jerusalem will come from the third heaven, where God dwells, and travel through space, and come near the earth and hover above the earth, for the next thousand years. After the millennium is fulfilled the New Jerusalem will now be placed as the capital upon the new earth. Jesus will speak and all of the new Heaven and new Earth will be moved into place and then exist forever. This heavenly city will be beautiful, beyond description, and perfect, in all appointments, like a bride presents herself perfect in poise and dress.

3. *And I heard a great voice out of heaven saying, Behold, the tabernacle of God is with men, and he will dwell with them, and they shall be his people, and God himself shall be with them, and be their God.*

Many times, in the book of Revelation, an angel from heaven announced an important message to man, about what God was doing in the fulfillment of the plan found in the Seven Scaled Book. The blessed news was that God would forever live with man, to be among them in a loving relationship. Starting from the beginning of the millennium all races of people, from around the world, including the people of Israel, shall be His people. God will be with all the redeemed, of the earth, and will be their God in a family relationship of a Father. God will forever continue to express His love and concern for those who are precious to Him. Ephesians 2:7 "That in the ages to come he might shew the exceeding riches of his grace in his kindness toward us through Christ Jesus."

4. *And God shall wipe away all tears from their eyes; and there shall be no more death, neither sorrow, nor crying, neither shall there be any more pain: for the former things are passed away.*

Believers will never experience an emotional circumstance with God that would bring tears, as a result of grief. Children of God will never die, nor have a loved one to die, and feel the loneliness and abandonment we experience on earth. The joyful feeling of worshiping our Lord, will never cease, because, forever Jesus is worthy of our praise and worship. Sorrow will not be known, where there is exultant joy, as a result of being with our Lord. A broken spirit causes the soul to cry out in desperation, of helplessness, and in heaven nothing will happen to bring such sorrow. Sickness and pain will not exist, because, every believer will have a glorified resurrected body, that will be perfect and, also, because God has taken all of these things away. Life as human beings know today, on this planet, shall be no more in heaven.

5. *And he that sat upon the throne said, Behold, I make all things new. And he said unto me, Write: for these words are true and faithful.*

The person of Jesus is the major theme of the book of Revelation. The one seated upon the throne, in heaven, is the Lord Jesus Christ. Jesus calls attention to the importance of the statement to follow, by saying, behold: which is to say pay attention, and listen attentively. The Holy Spirit knowing man may have some problems of understanding, some phenomenal event, may repeat the statement, to solidify that truth, in the mind of the skeptic. What God says is truth and it is never deceptive. God is always faithful to do precisely what He promises. What may seem difficult, or impossible, to a human being is the ability of God to create a new heaven and a new earth. The word new in this verse is the same Greek word for new in verse one, which has the idea of bringing into existence, something that did not exist and was something recently constructed.

6. *And he said unto me, It is done. I am Alpha ad Omega, the beginning and the end. I will give unto him that is athirst of the fountain of the water of life freely.*

Jesus the Saviour, of all mankind, announces it is done. First, we see that the redemption of the world has now been completed, and the world brought back under God's control; and second, it is done or it is certain, that there will be a new heaven and a new earth created, after the end of the tribulation period. At this time, in the study of Revelation, all things have been completed, to fulfill the judgments of God, and now it is time for bringing in the new earth and heaven. God once again pronounces His attribute of Eternity, by stating, He is the first and the last of all things. The mercy of God is extended to all people, today, to accept Jesus as their Lord and Saviour and by that be saved. Those who are thirsting to know the Lord as Saviour are invited to partake of salvation, in order, to satisfy the hearts innate desire to know God. To drink freely means that salvation is available to every one who desires to be saved.

7. *He that overcometh shall inherit all things; and I will be his God, and he shall be my son.*

Those who have overcome are all those who have trusted Jesus, by grace through faith, to be their Lord and Saviour. The things that shall be inherited are all things in heaven, and all things that belong to our Saviour. In the near future, the bride of Christ will have the privilege to sit with Christ in His throne, which means, we shall inherit all things that belong to the Bridegroom. Revelation 3:21 "To him that overcometh will I grant to sit with me in my throne, even as I also overcame, and am set down with my Father in his throne"

The promise is that God will be the Father, to all His children, with His divine quality of care and love for them. Our relationship to God is of that of a child who looks to Him for all things.

8. *But the fearful, and unbelieving, and the abominable, and murderers, and whoremongers, and sorcerers, and idolaters, and all liars, shall have their part in the lake which burneth with fire and brimstone: which is the second death.*

The Holy Spirit moved John, to list some of the characteristics, of the lost person who will die without Christ, and spend eternity in the lake of fire. The fearful would be those who were reluctant, to trust Jesus to save them, because of being timid about the change of their social life style, and circle of friends they would lose. The unbelieving are those who will not trust the Word of God, about salvation, and had rather remain a skeptic. The abominable are those who are so contaminated with sin, and as a result, cannot understand they are lost. The murderers have no regard for life, and kill for the thrill, or excitement, they may experience. A whore-monger is a person who does not control their sexual desires, and seeks physical pleasure, from many different people they may encounter. Sorcerers participate in the use of drugs, witchcraft, and magic for deceiving others. Idolaters devote their time, and attention, to other things, rather that to permit God, to have their first interest, and attention, in their life. All liars seek to deceive by hiding their sinful life, behind false statements, which make them appear to be decent citizens. Liars have no respect for truth, and have difficulty believing the truth, of the Word of God. All people who have this life style, reflect a wicked heart, and will be cast into hell. The lost people experience a second death, which is associated with the condition of the soul that is banished from God, with no hope of salvation, or to be delivered from the lake of fire.

9. *And there came unto me one of the seven angels which had the seven vials full of the seven last plagues, and talked with me, saying, Come hither, I will shew thee the bride, the Lamb's wife.*

Recorded, in chapter sixteen, is the account of the seven angels, who had seven bowls of judgments, to be poured out upon the world. One of these seven angels invited John to follow him, and he would be able, to see the Bride of Christ who was dwelling in the New Jerusalem. The bride of Christ is the New Testament Church, who was taken into heaven before the tribulation period started, and was married to Jesus in heaven. After the tribulation period is finished, the bride of Christ will return to the earth, and coming with the bride, will be their beautiful city Jesus has prepared for them. Justification declares the bride of Christ to be pure and white and clothed about with the righteousness of the Son of God. The bride will appear, in heaven, as holy and righteous as Jesus. Ephesians 5:27 "That he might present it to himself a glorious church, not having spot, or wrinkle, or any such thing; but that it should be holy and without blemish."

10. *And he carried me away in the spirit to a great and high mountain, and shewed me that great city, the holy Jerusalem, descending out of heaven from God.*

John describes the holy city, called the New Jerusalem, the size, liken to that of a great mountain. A mountain was the largest thing John could use, to describe something of the magnitude of the size of the city prepared, for the bride of Christ. Fourteen hundred miles square and fourteen hundred miles high was so extensive, that John could not express its size adequately. When Jesus comes to the earth, in His revelation, at the end of the tribulation, He will bring His bride and the city with Him. At first, the Holy City will hover above this earth, for the duration of the millennium. The city will be close to the earth, but will not touch the earth, that had been cursed, by God, when Adam fell into sin in the Garden of Eden. Micah 4: 1." But in the last days it shall come to pass, that the mountain of the house of the Lord shall be established in the top of the mountains, and it shall be exalted above the hills; and people shall flow unto it. 2. And many nations shall come, and say, Come, and let us go up to the mountain of the Lord, and to the house of the God of Jacob; and he will teach us of his ways, and we will walk in his paths: for the law shall go forth of Zion, and the word of the Lord from Jerusalem."

The rest of the book of Revelation describes the conditions of the New Jerusalem, being established, upon the new earth, after the end of the millennium. For all eternity, the New Jerusalem will be the capital of the whole new world.

From the throne within the city Jesus will be the Lord of lords and King of kings of the entire new world.

11. *Having the glory of God: and her light was like unto a stone most precious, even like a jasper stone, clear as crystal;*
Where Jesus is there is the shining of His Glory that radiates from His very being as God. The city is eternally lighted with the Glory of God and, it is a manifestation, of His divine attribute of Holiness. The color of light John saw was like, the light emitting from, the jasper stone. The colors of the jasper are translucent colors of blue, rose, and green. The light was most precious conveying the idea of something beautiful beyond human description.

12. *And had a wall great and high, and had twelve gates, and at the gates twelve angels, and names written thereon, which are the names of the twelve tribes of the children of Israel:*
In the Old Testament times cities had walls built, for protection, and they were ornaments of beautiful architecture, which added to the grandeur of the city. Each gate was a magnificent work of art which enhanced the craftsmanship, of the masons, of each city. The wall around the New Jerusalem will be for the enhancement, of the beauty, of the city. Within the walls of the city is a place, or a symbol, of security, for the bride of Christ, who uniquely belongs to the Lord Jesus. An angel sentinel is at each gate giving the idea of our Lord's watch care, and concern, of our Lord, for His bride, who dwells within the walls of the New Jerusalem. The names of the twelve tribes of Israel are inscribed upon each of the twelve gates.

13. *On the east three gates; on the north three gates; on the south three gates; and on the west three gates.*
There is a wall around the four sides of the city, and there are three gates, on each side of the four walls.

14. *And the wall of the city had twelve foundations, and in them the names of the twelve apostles of the Lamb.*

The Bible does not tell us about the distribution of the twelve foundations; it is assumed that there will be three foundations on each side of the four sides of the city. Foundations were made from large stones, placed below the surface of the land, and most often, would rest upon solid rock. Upon such foundations the building would rest securely for the structure to stand firm. A foundation is most important, in the structure of a wall, or building, and this foundation represents an important rock, upon which our Lord built His church. The foundations were named for the apostles, upon whom the Lord Jesus laid the foundation, for the ministry of the Gospel.

15. *And he that talked with me had a golden reed to measure the city, and the gates thereof, and the wall thereof.*

The one who was talking to John, is mentioned in verse nine, as one of the seven angels which poured out the vials of judgment on the earth. A golden reed, almost eleven feet long, signifies the value and importance of this measuring rod. A reed was used to measure long distances, and around great cities, and buildings. The dimensions of the city and wall are now given by the measuring with the reed.

16. *And the city lieth foursquare, and the length is as large as the breadth: and he measured the city with the reed, twelve thousand furlongs, The length and the breadth and the height of it are equal.*

The city, named the New Jerusalem, is in the form of a cube. Twelve thousand furlongs is the distance of 1378 to 1500 miles on each side and the height is also 1378 miles high. Some people have difficulty believing a city could reach such heights; since the base is of this distance and would be equal to the height, this as a result, would form a cube which would not be top heavy.

17. *And he measured the wall thereof, an hundred and forty and four cubits, according to the measure of a man, that is, of the angel.*

A cubit is the distance from the elbow to the end of the middle finger. Eighteen inches, times one hundred and forty and four, is seventy two yards high. Measuring in feet, the wall is two hundred sixteen feet high. The height of the wall is impressive, and will compliment the beauty of the New Jerusalem.

18. *And the building of the wall of it was of jasper: and the city was pure gold, like unto clear glass.*

The material which is built into the wall is that of jasper. A jasper stone is a translucent mineral with the hue of blue, rose, and green. The combination of colors could reflect the light of the holiness of God, and appear to be that of a rainbow. The New Jerusalem is constructed of pure gold. John describes the purity of the gold, by comparing it to clear glass, which has no impurities. The color of the city is a brilliant yellow that glows with the reflection of the glory of our Lord Jesus.

19. *And the foundations of the wall of the city were garnished with all manner of precious stones. The first foundation was jasper; the second, sapphire; the third, a chalcedony; the fourth, an emerald;*

There are twelve different foundations that support the wall of the city. Each foundation is a different stone, and sparkles, with the brilliant light from each color. The first foundation is the same, as the material, used to construct the wall with the color of green, blue, and rose. The second foundation was a sapphire with the violet blue color as known in Biblical days. Third, the chalcedony has a blue green color. The fourth was an emerald and a color of green and the Hebrew word indicates a shining glow from the stone.

20. *The fifth, sardonyx; the sixth, sardius; the seventh, chryso-lyte; the eighth, beryl; the ninth, a topaz; the tenth, a chrys-oprasus; the eleventh, a jacinth; the twelfth, an amethyst.*

The fifth stone is the sardonyx, with a red layer over a black layer, or some other colored layer. The sixth is a sardius with a deep red color. The seventh is chrysolyte with a yellow color. The eighth foundation is a beryl and the color is uncertain, although, a blue-green or turquoise has been suggested for this stone. The ninth is a topaz with a yellow-green color. The eleventh is a jacinth with a blue color or perhaps a yellow. The twelfth is an amethyst, which is a quartz stone, with a purple or violet color. With all of these different colors, reflecting the glorious light of the Glory of God, will be such a spectacular radiance, of color, shining forth from each foundation, that we shall forever be delighted, with what we shall behold in heaven, and the lights we shall see there.

21. *And the twelve gates were twelve pearls: every several gate was of one pearl: and the street of the city was pure gold, as it were transparent glass.*

Pearls in ancient days were considered to be more desirable than precious stones. Pearls were rare, and most requested, for making jewels. Each of the twelve gates had one pearl. The streets of the New Jerusalem were made of pure gold. The quality of the gold, in the streets, was as pure as clear glass. As it were transparent glass informs us that this is symbolic, it is glass without any impurities, or any added foreign material; Gold, therefore, is of the same quality as pure glass without any impurities or any foreign substances added to the gold.

22. *And I saw no temple therein: for the Lord God Almighty and the Lamb are the temple of it.*

John was looking upon the New Jerusalem the city of the bride of Christ. There was a temple in Heaven where God dwells. Hebrews 9:11 "But Christ being come an high priest of good things to come, by a greater and more perfect tabernacle, not made with hands, that is to say, not of this building:" In the New Jerusalem, situated upon the new earth, will no longer need a temple, as a place, where an atonement can be made, for the sins of man and where there is a mediator between God and man. The presence of the Lord God, and Jesus Christ, will always be in there midst and will become one holy temple where God and man dwell together.

23. *And the city had no need of the sun, neither of the moon, to shine in it: for the glory of God did lighten it, and the Lamb is the light thereof.*

Where Jesus is there is no darkness, because, His holy presence dispels all darkness. The Holiness of God is the effulgence of the radiance of His being. The light of the city will cover the whole earth and it will be lighted with the Holiness of God. Isaiah 60:19 "The sun shall be no more thy light by day; neither for brightness shall the moon give light unto thee: but the Lord shall be unto thee an everlasting light, and thy God thy glory. 20. Thy sun shall no more go down; neither shall thy moon withdraw itself: for the Lord shall be thine everlasting light, and the days of thy mourning shall be ended."

24. *And the nations of them which are saved shall walk in the light of it: and the kings of the earth do bring their glory and honour into it.*

In verse nine, one of the seven angels which had the vial judgments, showed John the holy city New Jerusalem. The time, when John saw the Lamb's wife, was during the millennium. The occasion, where the nations walk in the light of the New Jerusalem, is during the millennium. The nations are, in Greek, recorded as "Ethne" identifying them to be the Gentile people, who will be the bride of Christ. The kings of the earth are those believers, who have received their reward of holding an important office, of ruling, during the millennium. All inhabitants, who enter the New Jerusalem, will properly bring glory and honor into the city, with their praise and worship of the Lord Jesus, who is seated upon the throne, in the midst of the New Jerusalem.

25. *And the gates of it shall not be shut at all by day: for there shall be no night there.*

The New Jerusalem will never be closed. Everyone who has access to the city are those who have been redeemed, from the earth, by the shed blood of the sacrifice made by the Lord Jesus, on the cross. The city of God is the dwelling Jesus promised to prepare, for the New Testament Saints, in John 14:2 "In my Father's house are many mansions: if it were not so I would have told you. I go to prepare a place for you. 3. And if I go and prepare a place for you, I will come again, receive you unto myself; that where I am there ye may be also."

26. *And they shall bring the glory and honour of the nations into it.*

All during the time of the millennial kingdom Christians, from all gentile nations, will dwell in the New Jerusalem. The most wonderful and glorious worship will take place when all the diversity of different tribes, from around the world, worship the Lord and glorify Him in harmony and praise.

27. *And there shall in no wise enter into it any thing that defileth, neither whatsoever worketh abomination, or maketh a lie: but they which are written in the Lamb's book of life.*

No evil person, or fallen angel, will ever enter he city, our Lord has prepared for His bride. Any thing that defileth, or is unclean, because of the contamination of sin, will not enter the city of our Lord. The only one permitted to enter the city, through the gates, are those who have their sins blotted out by the blood of Jesus. Acts 3:19 "Repent ye therefore, and be converted, that your sins may be blotted out, when the times of refreshing shall come from the presence of the Lord;" Those who worketh abomination are wicked souls with a morally degraded nature and these shall not enter the city. Those who are morally good, but have refused to trust Jesus as their Saviour, will never approach the gates of the city of our Lord. Those who lie, and deceive, for the purpose of gaining access to the Holy city, will never enter the city. At the moment a person is born again, by receiving Jesus as their Lord and Master, will have their record of sin blotted out of the book of life, and their names recorded in the Lamb's book of life; they will be welcomed by Jesus to enter the Holy City.

Chapter XXII

Introduction: The first seven verses of this chapter, describe what is found in the New Jerusalem, and what will be the blessings for those who are the bride of Christ, and dwell there. John was so overwhelmed with what he saw, and heard, that he was moved to lie prostrate, in order to worship the Lord God of Heaven. John was once again instructed not to worship, at the feet of the angel, because it may appear that he was worshiping the angel. Verses eleven through verse seventeen are, the last appeal, and invitation for man to be saved, by the grace of God. Verses eighteen and nineteen, clearly, give a stern warning that if any person rejects any of the Word of God, or adds to what the Bible says, they will be lost and will never enjoy the blessings of Heaven.

1. *And he shewed me a pure river of water of life, clear as crystal, proceeding out of the throne of God and of the Lamb.*

　　The description of the New Jerusalem will be the same for the city during the millennium, and after the millennium is over, the city will settle down on the new earth. There is a throne of God in the center of the city, and out from under the throne, flows a pure river out of the city. The water in the river is clear as crystal, which could be interpreted, from the Greek, to be bright or sparkling water. Crystal is the purest of all glass, and like this the water is, also, pure. The throne of God and the Lamb, suggest that God the Father and God the Son will sit on the throne, in the New Jerusalem. Psalm

46:4 "There is a river, the streams whereof shall make glad the city of God, the holy place of the tabernacles of the most High."

2. *In the midst of the street of it, and on either side of the river, was there the tree of life, which bare twelve manner of fruits, and yielded her fruit every month: and the leaves of the tree were for the healing of the nations.*

The street, along side of the river, could be wide with a median separating the street. In the median, in the midst of the street, would have growing living trees. The river flows to the east from the throne. Ezekiel 47:8 "Then said he unto me, These waters issue out toward the east country, and go down into the desert, and go into the sea: which being brought forth into the sea, the waters shall be healed." The river flowing into the desert would place this occasion to be during the millennium, because, the new earth after the millennium will not be a desert to the east of Jerusalem, as it is today. On each side of the beautiful river, there will be fruit trees growing which bare a different fruit, for each of the twelve months of the year. The Bible does not say that we shall eat of the fruit of the trees, but it is obvious, that God gave the fruit for the purpose of eating.

In the garden of Eden God placed a tree bearing leaves, and if eaten, would assure that death would not come to those who eat. Genesis 3:22 "And the Lord God said, Behold, the man is become as one of us, to know good and evil: and now, lest he put forth his hand, and take also of the tree of life, and eat, and live for ever:" There will be human beings living during the millennium, and this is the reason, why there is a need for the tree of life, to sustain life for these human beings for all of the one thousand years.

3. *And there shall be no more curse: but the throne of God and of the Lamb shall be in it; and his servants shall serve him:*

At the time of the original creation there was no curse upon man, or the earth. The curse came because of man's disobedience, of the will of God for their lives. When man fell in the garden, the curse was pronounced upon man, and the earth, because, there is a penalty for all sins against God. Genesis 3:17 "And unto Adam he said, Because thou hast hearkened unto the voice of thy wife, and hast eaten of the tree, of which I commanded thee, saying, Thou shalt not eat of it: cursed is the ground for thy sake; in sorrow shalt thou eat of it all the days of thy life;" The original curse will be removed, after the millennium, and the blessings originally found in the garden of Eden, will now be experienced by the children of God.

The throne of God will be established in the millennium, and also, will forever be established in the new earth. Redeemed man will be with the Lord God, and the Lamb, never to be separated from His presence. The servants will be the host of heaven, including angels, who will serve the Lord by worshiping Him.

4. *And they shall see his face; and his name shall be in their foreheads.*

It is the face of a dear loved one that we desire to see most. All of the disciples looked upon the face of the Lord Jesus, when he was clothed about with a human body. On the mountain of Transfiguration, Peter, James, and John, were permitted to see the face of Jesus in His glorified state. Mark 9:2 "And after six days Jesus taketh with him Peter, and James, and John, and leadeth them up into a high mountain apart by themselves: and he was transfigured before them." The glow of the radiance of the Holiness was more than the human body was able to behold. When believers are resurrected, and receive their glorified bodies, we shall have the capacity to look upon the full radiance of His face, and be delighted to see that purity of His Holiness. The name in their foreheads is the sign of belonging, to the Lord Jesus. When a bride takes the name of her husband this identifies them as becoming one in the union of marriage. The marriage of the church to Jesus will make us, to become, one with Him and we shall bear his name, as belonging to Christ.

5. *And there shall be no night there; and they need no candle, neither light of the sun; for the Lord God giveth them light: and they shall reign for ever and ever.*

John once again informs us, that in heaven, where Jesus is present, there will be no darkness. The glorious light, from the presence of holiness, will fill all of heaven, and there will never be a need of any kind of light, to dispel darkness. The whole earth will be filled with the light of deity. I Timothy 6:16 "Who only hath immortality, dwelling in the light which no man can approach unto; whom no man hath seen, nor can see: to whom be honour and power everlasting. Amen." All creatures in heaven, will serve the Lord, and worship Him, through out all eternity, because, God the Father and Jesus the Son of God will forever be worthy, of praise from all of the heavenly hosts. There never will be a time when praise will cease, because, our Lord will forever be worthy of our praise.

6. *And he said unto me, These sayings are faithful and true: and the Lord God of the holy prophets sent his angel to shew which must shortly be done.*

What John has just written, about heaven, seems so wonderful, that some skeptics may think this could never happen. The angel tells John to write, once again, that the message he has just been given is true, and God is faithful to fulfill all that He has promised, even though, it may seem to be too good to be true. God in the past gave promises to the prophets, which at the time were to be fulfilled in the future, and in due time, God fulfilled all He promised and not one prophecy failed, to be fulfilled, just as God promised. Just as God said "all things prophesied to be fulfilled before the time of the rapture of the church has now been fulfilled."

7. *Behold, I come quickly: blessed is he that keepeth the sayings of the prophecy of this book.*

When the last judgment is poured out, by the seventh angel, the clear message is that Jesus will come back to this earth, in His revelation, to start the millennium. Blessed are those who are saved during the tribulation, and live until the start of the millennium, because, they will enter the millennium alive, and will live through the millennium. Near the end of the tribulation period it will be very difficult for the lost people to obey the prophecy of this book and trust Jesus to save them. This will be a time of great fear because of the power of the antichrist to destroy those who accept Jesus to be their Lord and Saviour.

8. *And I John saw these things, and heard them. And when I had heard and seen, I fell down to worship before the feet of the angel which shewed me these things.*

An angel took John and showed him the beautiful city, called the New Jerusalem. John saw the material used in the buildings and the streets. John had looked upon the pure light of the city which was the brightness of the Holiness of God. The emotions of excitement, were so intense, because of what John saw, and heard from the anthems of praise, that he could not refrain from the impulse to worship at the feet of the angel.

9. *Then saith he unto me, See thou do it not: for I am thy fellowservant, and of thy brethren the prophets, and of them which keep the sayings of this book: worship God.*

The angel rebuked John again for worshiping at his feet. Worshiping God is always in order, but never when it may appear that some angel, or person, is being worshiped. The angel gave John a reason why he must not worship at his feet; the angel said that he was not Deity just a fellowservant who is not any different than the prophets of God.

10. *And he saith unto me, Seal not the sayings of the prophecy of this book: for the time is at hand.*

Daniel ends his book by stating that the truths of prophesy may not be understood until the end times, or the time just before the start of the tribulation period. Daniel 12:9 "And he said, Go thy way, Daniel: for the words are closed up and sealed till the time of the end." John writes for students of the book of Revelation, who understand these truths, not to keep them secret, but to teach and warn about the impending judgments that will soon come during the tribulation. When people are understanding, and teaching, the book of Revelation, it would be a clear sign that the second coming of Jesus is near.

11. *He that is unjust, let him be unjust still: and he that is righteous, let him be righteous still: and he that is holy, let him be holy still.*

Before the final invitation is given, the Holy Spirit warns man that the lost soul will be forever lost, if they die in that lost condition. The born again believer dies as a saint of God and will never be lost. He that is unjust is the wicked person, who rejects Jesus as their Lord and Saviour. The filthy individual is vial, and impure, in thoughts and deeds. There is no second chance to be saved, after the lost individual dies. What a person is at the time of their death is what they will be for all eternity. Hebrews 9:27 "And as it is appointed unto men once to die, but after this the judgment:" The conclusion is, if you die lost, you will be judged at the Great White Throne Judgment; and if you die saved you will be judged, at the Judgment Seat of Christ.

12. *And, behold, I come quickly; and my reward is with me, to give every man according as his work shall be.*

The world will not be expecting the return of the Lord Jesus, when He comes to catch the church out of this world. The coming of Jesus is quick in that believers will be caught away in the rapture, before the world knows what is taking place. The reward is better understood, in the original language, of the Bible as wages. For believers, our wages are eternal life, with Jesus in heaven and for the lost, their wages are to be banished from God, and spend eternity in hell. Every person will receive justly what they have earned, although, believers will be given mercy instead of justice.

13. *I am Alpha and Omega, the beginning and the end, the first and the last.*

Jesus proclaims to John that He is the eternal God, Who is deity, and what He has always been He will always be, the immutable God.

14. *Blessed are they that do his commandments, that they may have right to the tree of life, and may enter in through the gates into the city.*

Most happy are they who do His commandments, which can be understood, as those who have washed their garments in the blood of the Lamb. Revelation 7:14 "And I said unto him, Sir, thou knowest. And he said to me, These are they which came out of great tribulation, and have washed their robes, and made them white in the blood of the Lamb." Doing the commandment of the Lord is trusting Jesus, by faith, to save them and cleanse them from all their sins

Two blessings are given to those who have received Jesus to save them. The first one is they will have access to the tree of life, and by eating of this tree they will live forever. The second is for believers to enter the New Jerusalem, through the beautiful gates, and have the privilege of enjoying the city the Lord Jesus has prepared for His Bride.

15. *For without are dogs, and sorcerers, and whoremongers, and murderers, and idolaters, and whosoever loveth and maketh a lie.*

The Lord had John to list some sins that are sure to destroy a soul, and be cast into hell. Those listed as dogs are Gentiles who have never been saved. Sorcerers are those who practice witchcraft, and become involved with drugs of all kind. Whoremongers are fornicators, and adulterers, who practice immorality as a way of life. Murderers kill other people for many reasons. Life comes from God and man is made in the image of God. The sanctity of life is to be preserved and honored. Idolaters include every one who devotes their interest to any thing more than to God which then becomes their idol. Every person who deceives lives a life of lies and God will judge those who take advantage of the innocent.

16. *I Jesus have sent mine angel to testify unto you these things in the churches. I am the root and the offspring of David, and the bright and morning star.*

The Lord Jesus sent an angel, as His messenger, to give testimony to the churches, about the authenticity of Jesus. The record of the lineage of Jesus identifies Him to be a descendant, of the family tree of David, and according to Scripture, to be the rightful heir to the throne of David. The prophecy of Isaiah was fulfilled, when Jesus was born of the seed of Jesse, who was the father of David. Isaiah 11:1 "And there shall come forth a rod out of the stem of Jesse, and a Branch shall grow out of his roots."

The bright and morning star is Jesus, the One who brought the gospel, and salvation, to a lost world. The brightness of Jesus dispels all darkness that dwells in the dark and sinful heart, when they trust Jesus to save them, by His grace.

17. *And the Spirit and the bride say, come. And let him that heareth say, Come. And let him that is athirst come. And whosoever will, let him take the water of life freely.*

The all inclusive invitation is given to a lost world to be saved. Truly, the Holy Spirit must convict the lost of their sins, and convince them to invite Jesus to come into their live and save them. The New Testament Church is the bride of Christ and today the church invites all sinners to be saved. If any person hears the gospel, they should respond to the good news of salvation for them to come and to be saved. Thirst is an urgent desire to be satisfied, and nothing else will meet that need. If a sinner realizes their lost condition, and desires to be satisfied, they are to come to Jesus, because, He is the only one who can satisfy the broken heart.

Any person who realizes they are lost and Jesus will save them is invited to come, to Jesus, who is the water that gives life Isaiah 55:1 "Ho, every one that thirsteth, come ye to the waters, and he that hath no money, come ye, buy, and eat; yea, come, buy wine and milk without money and without price."

18. *For I testify unto every man that heareth the words of the prophecy of this book, If any man shall add unto these things, God shall add unto him the plagues that are written in this book:*

The testimony of Jesus is very clear to every person who hears, or reads, the content of the Bible. Man is to accept the Bible, as given by the Holy Spirit, to be the infallible Word of God. The Bible is the complete word that God has given to man, and there does not need to be more, and if so, God would have breathed on men of God, to write more to the Scriptures. There are lost, arrogant intellectuals, who seek to display their superior mental capacity, by evaluating Scripture, and concluding that more needs to be added to what God has given. Adding to the Bible is to infer that God was limited in His ability to express His thoughts, and incapable of adequately stating the truth. The penalty of such presumption, on the part of man, is to be lost and stand before the Lord Jesus to be rejected, and cast into hell.

19. *And if any man shall take away from the words if the book of this prophecy, God shall take away his part out of the book of life, and out of the holy city, and from the things which are written in this book.*

Taking away any part of the Scripture is for that person to reject that segment as not truth, and was not breathed upon man, by the Holy Spirit. The haughty spirit of some individuals is so presumptuous not to trust God to say the truth, and they judge for themselves error, and reject some statements God recorded in the Bible. Those who deny, and reject, any of the Bible will never inter the holy city of life. Those literary critics will never enjoy the blessings of being with Jesus, and dwelling in the new earth, called heaven.

20. *He which testifieth these things saith, Surely I come quickly. Amen. Even so, come, Lord Jesus.*

Jesus is saying, to the students of this book, to take note about when the events of Revelation start, that His coming to the earth, will be in the short period of time, of seven years. Surely I come quickly is the promise Jesus made, that it is certain, He will come back to end the tribulation period. The amen confirms it is as God has promised, and in time will be fulfilled. Even so is for Christians to pray for the soon return of Jesus, and establish the Millennium, which will result in a government, of perfect rule over the whole earth.

21. *The grace of our Lord Jesus Christ be with you all. Amen.*

John starts the writing of the revelation, by pronouncing, a blessing upon those who read and study this book. Now, John is ending the book with another pronouncement of blessing upon all believers. The benediction is found in Paul's writings, and expresses, the divine Love of Jesus is to rest upon all Christians. This quality of divine love will forever be experienced by those who believe God's Word, and trust Jesus to be their Lord and Saviour. Amen expresses what was recorded in the book is to forever stand unchanged, or so be it as given.

CPSIA information can be obtained at www.ICGtesting.com
Printed in the USA
LVOW102234130712

290016LV00003B/1/P